Implementing

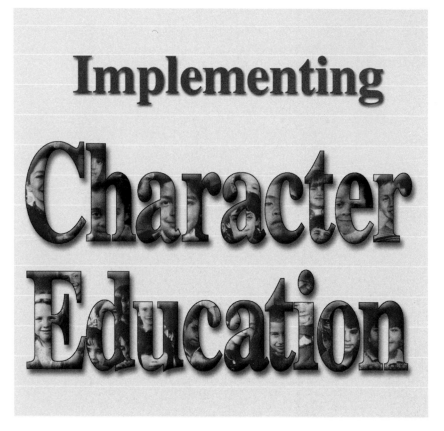

Character Education

MAY 1 6 2003

B. David Brooks, Ph.D.

Patricia Freedman, M.S.

Educational Assessment Publishing Company, Inc.

San Diego, California

Editorial Development: Heath Associates, Inc.
Art and Design: KenCom Graphics
Editor: David Heath
Cover Design: Lorie Kennedy

Printed and published in the United States of America.

ISBN 1-57279-253-1

1 2 3 4 5 6 7 8 9 — 07 06 05 04 03 02

Table of Contents

Introduction 1

Chapter 1 **The Reintroduction of Character Education** .3
Values Clarification Movement 4
Character Education Reintroduced 7
Character Education Defined 9
Analyzing a Character Education Program 11
Character Education Today 14
Case Study 15

Chapter 2 **The Need for Character Education** 19
Why Character Education? 22
Poor Character Affects Everyone 24
Negative and Positive Approaches 26
Positive Model for Change 27
Attitudes and Perceptions 29
Students Watch and Listen 30
Case Study 33

Chapter 3 **Planning and the Steering Committee** 35
Involve Everyone Early in the Process 35
Establishing the Steering Committee 38
Nine Essential Elements for Success 39
Defining Committee Members' Responsibilities .40
Setting Specific Program Goals 42
Categories of Goals 44
The Importance of Communication 47
Case Study 49

Chapter 4 **Assessing Your School's "Character Climate"** 53
Identify the Stakeholders 54
Assessing Attitudes 56
Assess Student Behaviors 61
A Character Skills Survey 62
Case Study 63

Chapter 5 **Language, Principles, and Practice** 65
Stages of Language Acquisition and Use 65
Literal Language and Thinking 67
The Three P's 71
Principles 73
Practice 77
Process 78
Case Study 79

Chapter 6 **The S.T.A.R. Decision-Making Process** 83
    The First Step: STOP 84
    The Second Step: THINK 86
    The Third Step: ACT 89
    The Fourth Step: REVIEW 93
    Using the Process 96
    Case Study 97

Chapter 7 **Implementation in the School** 99
    Climate and Environment 100
    Restructuring the Environment 103
    Advertising, Language, and Character 106
    School as an Island 107
    Signage 108
    Student Organizers 112
    Rules and Expectations 112
    Recognition 115
    The Character Moment 116
    Announcements 117
    Adult Modeling 118
    Some Final Thoughts 119
    Case Study 120

Chapter 8 **Connecting School, Parents, and Community** 123
    Involving Parents 123
    Helping Parents to Be Character Educators 127
    Parents as Community Resources 128
    Involving the Community 130
    Case Study 133

Chapter 9 **Evaluation** 137
    Establishing an Evaluation Procedure 139
    A Review of Some of the Research 145
        The Monk Study 145
        The Thorfinnson Study 145
        The Lein Study 146
        The Wulf Study 146
        The DeVargas Study 148
    What the Studies Show 149
    Case Study 152

Chapter 10 **Strategies for Maintaining Momentum** 155
    School Climate Strategies 156
    Classroom Strategies 159
    Parent and Community Involvement Strategies 162
    Guidance and Extracurricular Strategies 163
    Case Study 165

Endnotes for the Chapters 168

Appendices
    Appendix A: Character Education Survey 170
    Appendix B: Student Character Education Survey 172
    Appendix C: Organizations Involved with Character Education 174
    Appendix D: Funding Resources 176
    Appendix E: Selected Bibliography 178
    Appendix F: Grand Forks Timeline, Goals, and Budget 180

Index 184

Introduction

If we have learned anything in our combined half-century-plus work in the educational arena, it is that programs come and go but only last when there is an ongoing, systematic effort to maintain the program. Far too often, important educational innovations are implemented without appropriate planning and little follow-up. When this happens, the best of programs and intentions drift away and, unfortunately, the schools return to what has always been.

With all of the above in mind, we have written this book as a resource to assist you in planning, implementing, and maintaining an effective and enduring character education program. We want you to establish a character development effort that can grow, flourish, and achieve the goal of assisting students as they become responsible, respectful, caring, and productive citizens.

Before we began writing this book, we made some assumptions to guide us in our attempt to support you as you plan to implement or enhance a character education program.

We assume:

- All adults working with students are character educators. In other words, bus drivers, crossing guards, cafeteria workers, office personnel, aids, classroom teachers, counselors, coaches, and administrators model and teach character.

- Good teachers have always included character education as part of the life of the school or classroom.

- The purpose of formal education is to teach students academic subjects and, equally important, to teach them to be good people.

- Character education is primarily the responsibility of the home. Nevertheless, the school has the responsibility and the opportunity to support the efforts in the home and/or introduce the habits of good character in cases where the home has failed to do so.

- The habits of good character do not just happen. The principles, practices, and processes for developing good character must be taught.

- The most effective character education occurs when the entire school community is involved. All adults, parents, students, and the community at large must play a part in creating a school climate that supports the development of the habits of good character.

- Effective character educational efforts must include modeling, visuals, curricular inclusion of character principles, processes for helping students make ethical decisions, recognition of practices of good character, and evaluation.

These assumptions are basic to the implementation of a systematic character education program.

There are two other considerations that also come into play when a character development program is being developed, implemented or enhanced.

First, we know that each of us has a story of something that was said to us or about us by an educator. Along with parents, educators have a unique influence and power—both positive and negative—over the character development of students. For the rest of his or her life, a student may remember an off-handed remark, a pat on the back, a sarcastic comment, a smile of encouragement, or a caring attitude of an adult. You never know when you are going to have a life-long effect on a student. A school-wide systematic character education program can be a continual reminder of how we as educators influence the character growth of students.

Second, we believe: educators shape students' character every day in every way by what they do and what they say.

We wish you the best in your efforts to assist your students on their journey to becoming responsible, caring, respectful, civil, individuals who embrace and practice both the rights and responsibilities of citizenship.

We have written this book for you.

B. David Brooks and Pat Freedman

CHAPTER 1

The Reintroduction of Character Education

"Though schools must be neutral with respect to religion, they may play an active role with respect to teaching civic values and virtue, and the moral code that holds us together as a community. The fact that some of these values are held also by religions does not make it unlawful to teach them in schools.[1]"

United States Department of Education

Imagine it is 1989, and you are in charge of arranging an educational conference for your professional association. The chances are that you would probably not be looking for presenters on the subject of character education. Actually, if you did have a breakout session on character education or values in the schools, it would be sparsely attended. Attention to character education has increased during the last decade and continues to gain momentum. Many educators are interested in systematic character education but are unsure of how to proceed. This chapter will give you background on the character education movement and provide you with an understanding of its basic concepts.

During the early part of the 1980s, educators and parents began asking two major questions. The first focused on the growing fear that schools and families were losing the battle to raise responsible and respectful children. For the first time, parents and teachers became fearful of their children in the family and classroom. Adults began to fear what

American youth were doing to themselves and what the youth might do to the adults. Street gangs, teen pregnancy, an epidemic of drug and alcohol abuse, dropouts, runaways, and disrespect for parents and teachers led responsible adults to ask, "Where have we gone wrong?" This question lead to a second: "What can we do to stem the tide of violence, abuse, apathy, and lack of respect?"

A growing problem of negative student behaviors led to a variety of intervention programs.

These concerns were addressed with a plethora of programs focused on symptoms of this youth epidemic. Milk cartons carried the faces of children who, for the most part, were runaways. Intervention programs for teen pregnancy, drug abuse, and gang violence were funded with millions of dollars through local, state, and federal grants. Yet, the problems continued to grow through the 1980s and into the 1990s.

Values Clarification Movement

Coinciding with this emphasis on symptoms was the growth of the "values clarification" movement, which was also known as "moral relativism." Christina Sommers, in her essay, "Ethical Relativism: Teaching the Virtues" presents a succinct explanation of values clarification. She explains:

> How Not To Teach Ethics: One favored method of moral education that has been popular for the past twenty years is called "values clarification," which maintains the principle that the teacher should never directly tell students about right and wrong; instead, the students must be left to discover "values" on their own. One favored values clarification technique is to ask children about their likes and dislikes; to help them become acquainted with their personal preferences. The teacher asks the students questions like, "How do you feel about homemade birthday presents?" "Do you like wall-to-wall carpeting?" "What is your favorite color?" "Which flavor of ice cream do you prefer?" "How do you feel about hit-and-run drivers?" "What are your feelings on the abortion

question?" The reaction to these questions—from wall-to-wall carpeting to hit-and-run drivers—is elicited from the student in the same tone of voice, as if one's personal preferences in both instances are all that matter.[2]

Sommers argued that the educators have knowledge about morals and values and should impart that knowledge directly to students. She continues by stating:

> Some opponents of directive moral education argue that it could be a form of brainwashing. That is a pernicious confusion. To brainwash is to diminish someone's capacity for reasoned judgement. It is perversely misleading to say that helping children to develop habits of truth telling or fair play threatens their ability to make reasoned choices. Quite the contrary: Good moral habits enhance one's capacity for rational judgments.[3]

In My Experience

B. David Brooks: In the early 1980s, during the height of the values clarification era I served on a committee to review elementary reading books for the Los Angeles County Office of Education in California. My task was to look for character content in the stories. One of the stories presented in a primary grade basal reading series was the classic, *The Little Engine That Could*. Basically, there are two primary lessons or morals in this familiar story. One, of course, is related to the value of persevering. The engine struggling to climb the mountain while saying, "I think I can. I think I can." illustrates this value. The second, less obvious lesson in the story is related to what the train is carrying. It carries "Toys for good little boys and girls."

In reviewing this classic story, I found that the publishers had altered the text. The little engine was still trying to get somewhere and it did keep trying. However, for some reason, the mountain was removed from the story. The engine was now simply pulling the train "along the tracks."

Additionally, the shipment on the train, toys for good little boys and girls, was written into the story to teach a lesson. The point is, if you do good things, rewards, toys in this case, will come your way. The toys on the train were for *good* little boys and girls. Unfortunately, the editor removed the reference to *toys* and *good* little boys and girls and replaced this reference with the simple statement that the train was "carrying a cargo."

The committee, of course, rejected this version of the story because the essence of the story had been removed. We questioned why the editors felt it was necessary to eliminate the values lessons from this example of classic literature. We concluded that, in this era of values clarification, the publisher did not want to offend lazy children or boys and girls who were not good.

For me, this was a clear example of how far the educational establishment, including educational writers, publishers, and consumers had bought into the values clarification movement.

During the same period, a few educators began to view these interventions and their emphasis on values clarification as seriously flawed. It became obvious to educational practitioners and to those in the helping professions that any program focusing totally on symptoms and ignoring root causes was bound to fail. These individuals believed there was a need for prevention as well as intervention. They stressed that intervention was not the only (or even the most productive) answer to the epidemic of problems facing the youth of the day. They believed that prevention, not brief interventions, was critical to a long-term solution of these problems. At the center of this discussion was the premise that many of the difficulties encountered by youth stemmed from a lack of "character." Character development was viewed by prevention advocates as the primary method for helping individuals make informed, ethical decisions and thereby stem the growth of youth problems facing the nation.

Character Education Reintroduced

This thinking led to the publication in 1983 of *The Case for Character Education*[4], the first book to call for a systematic return to the teaching of core consensus values in homes and classrooms. The book detailed the pressures faced by youth and emphasized the compelling necessity for prevention by reintroducing systematic character education in the nation's schools.

These calls for systemic character education (also called "values education") as a primary tool for turning the tide met with disdain and apathy. When approached, many parents and educators clearly disapproved of the idea that teachers would be able to or responsible for teaching values to their students.

The litany of reasons why schools should stay out of the character education business was repeated in schools and communities across the nation. Heated debates in school auditoriums and boardrooms centered on several recurring themes. Those opposed to the schools' role in teaching values vehemently argued that:

- Character or values education is the responsibility of the home and the church.

- We, the family, already teach good character, and we do not need a special emphasis in our public schools and classrooms.

- Whose values will the teachers teach?

- There is not enough time; teachers' plates are already too full.

- We cannot teach values in our district because parents will object.

- If we try to do this in our school, the staff will revolt.

- We have no problem at this school; our students are respectful and responsible.

In spite of objections like these, a gradual awareness and acceptance began to spread of the need to consider systematic character education as an important educational tool. The critics remained vocal and persistent, but in spite of this resistance, more and more people began to accept the fact that youth problems were out of control. This awareness fueled a search for a way to assist children in avoiding these problems instead of waiting for the symptoms to emerge—drug abuse, teen pregnancy, dropping out of school, gang violence—and then trying to correct it.

Throughout the decade of the 1990s, character education gained momentum and support from the public, schools, and government.

There was agreement on one facet of the debate. Both sides agreed that the home is the primary place for teaching values. Nonetheless, those supporting the reintroduction of systematic character education pointed out that schools have always been partners with parents in helping students develop skills and habits of good character. They also argued that during the time values clarification dominated educational thinking, much of the emphasis on overt or systematic character development in the school diminished. Proponents of values clarification put forth the notion that each person developed his or her own values, and teachers should not impose any standards or their own values upon their students. This led to the demise of systematically including character or values as an element of the curriculum.

The publication of *Educating for Character*[5] in 1991 marked a turning point in the struggle to have educators seriously consider the importance of moving character education from the invisible curriculum to the visible. At about the same time, major educational journals and organizations began to explore the importance of character education. As awareness grew, urban, suburban, and rural school districts began to consider implementing character education programs.

As the momentum grew, character educators began to form organizations and associations dedicated to fostering the idea that schools could and should systematically teach values and character. Consequently, the resistance to the reintroduction of systematic character education began to wane. Coalitions such as The Character

Education Partnership, The Character Education Network of the Association of Supervision and Curriculum Development (ASCD), and The Character Counts! Coalition brought the issue of character education from the background to the foreground and helped to lend credibility to the role of schools in helping students develop the habits of good character.

Character Education Defined

Dr. Tom Lickona, in his book *Educating for Character*, defines character in several ways. He sums up his definition: "Character consists of operative values, values in action." He continues, "Character so conceived has three interrelated parts: moral knowing, moral feeling, and moral behavior. Good character consists of knowing the good, desiring the good, and doing the good—habits of the mind, habits of the heart, and habits of action."[6]

In *The Content of America's Character*, Don Eberly concludes:

> "To possess and live out good character, the individual must desire the good, must be aware of specific moral qualities that are expected in a character-centered society, and must be able to apply these qualities to concrete cases through rational, moral decision-making."[7]

The Character Education Partnership (CEP) has taken the definition of character education a step further by defining character education from an implementation point of view. This definition suggests how character, as defined above, will look when implemented in a classroom or school. CEP published "Eleven Principles of Effective Character Education,"[8] addressing character from a broader perspective. The preface states, "There is no single script for effective character education, but there are some important basic principles. The following eleven principles serve as criteria that schools and other groups can use to plan a character education effort and to evaluate available character education programs, books, and curriculum resources."

The different definitions of character education contain the same core beliefs.

1. Character education promotes core ethical values as the basis of good character.

2. "Character" must be comprehensively defined to include thinking, feeling, and behavior.

3. Effective character education requires an intentional, proactive, and comprehensive approach that promotes the core values in all phases of school life.

4. The school must be a caring community.

5. To develop character, students need opportunities for moral action.

6. Effective character education includes a meaningful and challenging academic curriculum that respects all learners and helps them succeed.

7. Character education should strive to develop students' intrinsic motivation.

8. The school staff must become a learning and moral community in which all share responsibility for character education and attempt to adhere to the same core values that guide the education of students.

9. Character education requires moral leadership from both staff and students.

10. The school must recruit parents and community members as full partners in the character-building effort.

11. Evaluation of character education should assess the character of the school, the school staff's functioning as character educators, and the extent to which students manifest good character.

As you can see, there are a number of definitions for character education. Throughout our book, we have defined character education in the following manner:

Character education is the systematic, purposeful teaching of core consensus values that leads to habits of good character. This involves the teaching of the Three P's. The first P, *principles*, consists of character traits such as civility, respect, caring, fairness, trustworthiness, responsibility, loyalty, and self-control, among others. The second P, *practices*, involves the translating of the principles into behavior or actions and ultimately habits of good character. The third P, *process* provides the individual with the necessary skills for making ethical decisions, resolving conflicts, and goal-setting.

Analyzing a Character Education Program

Based on a synthesis of the various definitions of character education, the following criteria has been developed to be used when reviewing character education programs, activities and related curriculum.

The following questions can be utilized as a checklist for determining the viability of programs or curricula. These questions can also be used to evaluate the effectiveness of an ongoing program in a school or district.

Criteria For Analysis of Character Education Programs

Principles

- Are the principles of good character clearly articulated?

- Is there an agreed-upon list of commonly held principles available to the staff and community?

- Is there a systematic lesson plan for teaching each principle?

- Are the principles taught consistently at each grade level?

- Is there a process for infusing the teaching of the principles into the general curriculum?

- Is there a plan to infuse the principles into the school at large?

Practices

- Are there clearly understood practices (observable behaviors) that are known to the students and staff?

- Are there lessons and activities available for students in order to assist them in translating the principles into actions?

- Are there activities for groups, classrooms, clubs, and/organizations that can be utilized to foster practicing behaviors related to the principles.

- Are there activities or evaluation instruments that will enable students to evaluate how effectively they are integrating the practices into their daily lives?

- Is there an instrument for evaluating student performance by staff related to practicing good character?

- Is there a procedure for informing parents of successful practices of individual students or students in general?

- Is there a procedure for evaluating and reporting of the progress of the school population related to practicing the habits of good character?

- Is there a procedure for identifying and rewarding success in the practice of the principle for individual students?

- Is there a procedure for identifying and rewarding success in the practice of the principles by classrooms, organizations, or other student groups?

Process

- Is there a clearly stated process for problem-solving, decision-making, conflict resolution, and goal-setting in place as part of the character education program?

- Are there lesson plans for infusing the process for problem solving, decision-making, conflict resolution, and goal-setting into the school culture outside of the classroom?

- Is there a process that can be utilized in the classroom as well as areas such as guidance, counseling, and disciplinary matters?

- Are parents aware of the process if one exists?

- Is there a program or procedure for teaching parents the process?

- If a process does exist, can it be infused into the general curriculum?

- Can students and staff articulate the steps in the process?

General

- Has the district administration taken part in developing the list of agreed-upon principles?

- Has the board of education taken part in the development of the list of agreed-upon principles?

- Is the character education effort school-wide?

- Is there visual evidence—posters, signs, etc.—that demonstrate that the school is committed to character education?

- Is there provision for inclusion of non-teaching staff in teaching, recognizing, supporting, and reinforcing the elements of the character education program?

- Is there a connection between the character education effort and other programs such as school-to-work or service learning?

- Is the community at large aware of the character education program?

- Is there a method defined for connecting character traits to the regular curricular content?

Character Education Today

In an April 2001 Issue Paper distributed by the Education Commission of the States[9] and the Character Education Partnership, character education is summarized in the following manner:

> Character education is a national movement to create schools that foster ethical, responsible, and caring young people by modeling and teaching good character. The emphasis is on common values such as respect, honesty, fairness, compassion, responsibility, civility, courage, and kindness. The goal is to help students develop socially, ethically, and academically by infusing character development into every aspect of the school culture and curriculum.[10]

By following the procedures outlined in this book, systematic character education can be successfully incorporated into a school or district

One measure of how character education is growing is the number of states that have passed legislation. As of January 2001, nine states and Puerto Rico have mandated character education through legislation, and eleven more states plus the District of Columbia have policies that recommend some form of character education (Education Commission of the States, 2001). Another measure of the growing recognition of character education is its rising prominence on the national scene. Miss America 2001, Angela Perez Baraquio, chose character education and the teachers responsible for it as the centerpiece of her platform. Moreover, in his first week in office, President George W. Bush released his education plan, which calls for increased funding for character education as part of the effort to encourage safe schools.

The time is long past for debating whether educators can or should be in the business of reintroducing systematic character into the classrooms. Systematic character education has now been accepted by educators, parents, politicians, and business leaders as a fundamental tool in the increasingly difficult task of raising and educating children and youth. The need for character is widely recognized. The job that remains is the infusing of systematic character education in every aspect of the educational experience.

For many in education, the societal and educational changes detailed above have set the stage for implementing a systematic character education program in their schools or districts. However, some who are ready to begin are not sure of the steps they must take to ensure success. The following chapters will provide documents, methods, and procedures that will guide you through this trip and help you avoid the roadblocks that loom ahead.

CASE STUDY

In 1996, the Humble Independent School District in Texas initiated a successful pilot program on two elementary school campuses in grades 4 and 5. Beginning in 1997–98 the district began dual implementation in all district schools. By 2000–2001, the entire district—K–12—was participating in the Humble Character Development Program.

The program has been evaluated against the Criteria for Analysis of Character Education Programs. In all categories, principles, practices, process, and general, the Humble Character Development Program rated "positive" in over 90 percent of the questions posed by the analysis.

Here are a few examples:

Principles

Q: Is there an agreed upon list of commonly held principles available to the staff and community?

A: Yes. The character education steering committee researched various programs and developed a list which includes: trustworthiness, respect, responsibility, random acts of kindness, fairness, caring, citizenship, and community service.

Q: Is there a plan to infuse the principles into the school at large?

A: Yes. The district has provided extensive signage for each school. In addition, the district has adopted a month-by-month schedule with each month dedicated to one of the principles. All district schools conduct classroom and school activities in support of the monthly theme.

Practice

Q: Are there clearly understood practices that are known to the students?

A: Yes. The district adopted the Six Pillars of Character[11] and added three of their own. Each school was provided a packet of materials that articulated specific strategies to assist students in the development of habits of good character.

Process

Q: Is a clearly stated process for problem solving, decision-making, and conflict resolution in place as part of the character education program?

A: Yes. The first month of each school year is dedicated to the S.T.A.R. process, which is a method for making decisions, solving academic problems, planning for the future, and resolving conflicts.

General

Q: Is there provision for inclusion of non-teaching staff in teaching, recognizing, and reinforcing the elements of the character education program?

A: Yes. During the 2000–2001 school year, all district bus drivers received a half-day of staff development centered on the district's character education goals and procedures. Each bus is equipped with a sign emphasizing the monthly theme and S.T.A.R.

Q: What part has the board of education taken in the development of the list of principles?

A: The administration and board drafted a resolution for character education, approved the list of themes, and adopted district goals related to character education. The five district goals are:

1. All district personnel will respect students, as well as expect students to respect them.

2. All district personnel will model behavior reflective of Humble ISD's six core principals and will expect students to display these same behaviors.

3. The Humble ISD Character Development Program will reinforce and promote good citizenship.

4. Parents and community members will participate in and support the Humble ISD Character Development Program.

5. The Six Pillars of Character will be embedded into all curricular areas, as well as into all school-based programs and activities.

By asking and answering the questions provided in the analysis, the district personnel were able to understand where they were in relation to systematic character education and to use this information to plan where and how they wanted to proceed with total implementation. This information also gave them valuable data for dissemination throughout the district.

CHAPTER 2

The Need for Character Education

❝For many years, our schools have majored in the "three Rs": Reading, (W)Riting and (A)Rithmetic. It is past time for three more Rs: Restraint Respect and Responsibility. These three virtues constitute the heart and core of essential character education virtues.[1]❞

Harry S. Dent

Traversing the road from childhood to adulthood has never been without its roadblocks, potholes, detours, and other obstacles that slow or reroute the traveler. For the youth traveling this road during the last quarter of the twentieth century and first few years of the twenty-first, this trip has been and will continue to be exceedingly difficult. There hasn't been any fundamental change in human nature. The path has been made more difficult because of a dramatic change in the ways in which children and adolescents receive information about who they are or who they should be.

Although the purpose of this book is to look at ways to help youth shape their lives in a positive way, there is value in briefly discussing some of the negative influences that make systematic character education vitally important. If, as many agree, we have a problem with cheating, apathy, violence, drug and alcohol abuse, and other manifestations of youthful discord, then as parents and as educators, we have both the responsibility and opportunity to do all we can to assist youngsters to become responsible citizens.

In this chapter, we will look at some of the factors influencing youth today. More importantly, however, we will focus on ways in which systematic character education can counter negative conditions retarding the development of habits of respectful and responsible living.

Today's students face a wide range of problems, and they need help addressing them.

There have been numerous studies and reports about the economic and social trends dating back to the 1960s. William Bennett has published a list of "leading cultural indicators,"[2] which gives a fairly clear picture of the changes in the climate in which children are living today.

United States Trends and Cultural Indicators 1960 – 1990

General Social Trends:

U.S. Population	Up 41%
Gross domestic product	Up 270%
Government social spending	Up 550%
Spending on welfare	Up 630%
Spending on education	Up 225%

Cultural Indicators:

Rate of illegitimate births	Up 419%
Children on welfare	Up 340%
Children living with single parents	Up 300%
Violent crime rate	Up 470%
Teen suicide rate	Up 200%

Although this information may seem somewhat outdated, it does indicate the gradual change in the factors that continue to influence the lives of children and adolescents today. The good news is that recent indicators are showing that crime in cities is on the decline. However, the bad news is that crime in schools—especially violent crime and behavior such as bullying—has remained the same or is increasing.

IN MY EXPERIENCE

B. David Brooks: I recently surveyed 831 educators who attended several of my presentations. While this was not a "strict" scientific study, the results do indicate that educators believe that the students entering their schools and classrooms are less respectful, more combative, more likely to show verbal and even physical disrespect, and are more inclined to lie, cheat, and steal than students in the past.

The informal survey asked participants to react to the following statements:[3]

Comparing students today with students you have had in the past, please indicate your responses on the one-to-five scale below. One (1) indicates you strongly disagree and five (5) indicates you strongly agree.

Please answer these questions by considering youth in general not the students with whom you interact in your school or classroom.

Statement	Average response
Students are trustworthy.	2.0
Students are responsible even when they are not being monitored.	1.9
Students are respectful toward staff.	2.3
Students react respectfully when disciplined.	2.3
Students view discipline codes, rules, and procedures as fair.	2.5

The survey consisted of 35 statements of this nature (See Appendix A). The sample statements above are typical of the perceptions of current day educators. The average response for the 831 surveys was 2.6. This indicates that approximately half of the persons surveyed felt that their students are not very trustworthy, responsible, or respectful.

Admittedly, this is not a scientific study, and the results should be taken in that light. Nevertheless, the responses do demonstrate that there is a perception on the part of educators that indicates they believe there is a lack of character on the part of youth in general.

Why Character Education?

In *Cultivating Heart and Character*, Devine, Seuk, and Wilson point out the following:

> A wide array of scholars, including Robert Bellah, Christopher Lasch, and Roy Baumeister, think the decline of explicit moral teachings in the last fifty to seventy-five years has left individuals with a "value gap" —no moral base on which to build a philosophy of life. Children are left to construct their own value system or even to avoid the task altogether. Without dedicated and consistent guidance, teenagers often adopt bits and pieces of values and goals from various sources, then to a large extent resort to personal satisfaction as their guiding orientation. Schools, home, and community owe it to young people to provide an explicit and consistent moral message so that popular, commercial culture and happenstance do not fill in the gap. Schools have traditionally played a key role in this socialization process, and their input is more crucial now than ever before.[4]

Systematic character education reinforces positive behaviors in all students, especially those who display negative behaviors.

Why is the role of the school so crucial now? Before we can answer that question, it is important to remind ourselves that the school is only one partner in this difficult undertaking. The home is the primary place for helping children develop the habits of good character. Yet we clearly know that the school can play a significant role in this regard. Lloyd V. Hackley, former chancellor of both Fayetteville State University in North Carolina and the University of Arkansas at Pine Bluff, states this unequivocally: "Education is of no value to this nation or humanity if it does not identify, expose, clarify, and transmit the core shared values that undergrid America."[5]

Whether we like it or not, many of the children entering schools are doing so without a basic understanding of the principles and practices of good character. This is not occurring because parents are bad or families are broken. The simple fact is: many parents lack the requisite skills to teach manners and values. In families wherein the skills for imparting these ideas are present, there simply may not be enough time to do so. Many parents are leaving the home before their children in the morning and are not returning until long after the children are home.

IN MY EXPERIENCE

Patricia Freedman: I recently asked a group of teachers if they thought the majority of the children they teach ate dinner at the dinner table at least five nights a week with the entire family. Only one or two thought that was the case. I continued to ask. Four nights a week? Three nights a week? It was clear as I went through this process that the vast majority of the teachers believed that the evening meal was not a part of the daily life of their students.

This underscored a problematic situation. Historically, for many families at least, it was during mealtime, especially supper that many of the value lessons were taught.

For many children and adolescents, the school has become the common denominator when it comes to the teaching of such concepts and skills as honesty, respect, caring, responsibility, and civility.

If, in fact, some of the primary familial interactions and lessons have disappeared from the lives of many youngsters, where are they learning the principles, practices, and processes for living a responsible and civil life? Unfortunately, many of the lessons in life to which youth are exposed are not lessons that will lead them toward civility or responsibility.

Let us be clear, we are not suggesting that all or even a majority of youth are evil, disrespectful, irresponsible, or lacking in character. That would not be a fair or accurate conclusion. There are more examples of caring, respectful, and responsible actions by children and adolescents in any given day in any classroom or school than examples of behaviors demonstrating lack of character. The problem is not that the majority of students are going in a wrong direction. The problem is that the number of students who display a lack of character is growing, and the acting out of behaviors associated with poor character are becoming increasingly serious.

Poor Character Affects Everyone

As the number of violent, disruptive, disrespectful, and irresponsible behaviors grows, it is apparent that not only the students who display poor character are affected. These actions also disrupt the opportunity for other students to participate in the learning process. It is not possible for students who are being mercilessly teased or bullied to fully participate in their education. It is not possible for a teacher who must spend a disparate amount of time disciplining a minority of students to fully engage the majority in the teaching/ learning process. It is not possible for a counselor or administrator who is buried by an avalanche of disciplinary referrals to adequately work with students who have other legitimate educational needs.

> Negative behaviors are becoming more serious and often violent.

The impact of the relatively small number of students who display poor character has a disproportionate effect on the educational process. For this reason, it is important that educators address character education in a proactive manner that emphasizes teaching and learning the skills of good character. This definitely constitutes the prevention philosophy mentioned in chapter one.

Some ask, "Is there really a problem?" The Report Card on the Ethics of American Youth,[6] which surveyed 8,600 students, reports the following:

Cheating

- 71% of all high school students admit they cheated on an exam at least once in the past 12 months.

- 45% said they cheated two or more times.

Lying

- 92% lied to their parents in the past 12 months.

- 79% lied to their parents two or more times.

- 78% lied to a teacher.

- 58% lied to a teacher two or more times.

- 27% said they would lie to get a job.

Stealing

- 40% of males and 30% of females say they stole something from a store in the past 12 months.

Drunk at School

- 61% say they have been drunk in school during the past year.

- 9% were drunk two or more times.

Propensity Toward Violence

- 68% hit someone because they were angry in the past year.

- 46% hit someone out of anger at least twice.

- 47% of all students said they could get a gun if they wanted to.

- 60% of male students said they could get a gun if they wanted to.

In examining the character of youth today, there is no dearth of data indicating that things are not as good as we would like them to be. When it comes to the character of today's youth, the general perception is that youth are troubled or in trouble. The real question each educator and parent must ask is how all this affects his or her school or district. There is no doubt that there are schools that *do not* have the problems listed above. Nonetheless, character education is still necessary in those schools. "Not my kids! Not my school!" is no longer a valid assumption.

Every school and every community is at risk. Character education is a safety net and can substantially reduce this risk.

Negative and Positive Approaches

If we assume that there are problems, some greater than others, then it follows that we, as educators, have some responsibility to look for solutions. For a moment, let's look at the model educators have generally used to solve building or district problems.

> Emphasizing the negative aspects of a situation can often hinder the search for a positive solution.

One very familiar scenario plays out like this: The general feeling at Bruce Street School is one of despair and a general belief that the kids do not care, are disrespectful, and behave irresponsibly. Because of this malaise, the administration calls an extended staff meeting and announces an attempt to turn things around. The staff is then divided into small groups. Each group gets a large piece of newsprint, pins it to the wall, and commences to make list of all the student-related problems that come to mind. After each group completes the task of listing the negative behaviors and everything else that is causing this despondency, they reconvene as a full staff and create a single list of the problems at the school. They then prioritize the list and develop a plan for "getting rid" of the most serious problems.

Think about this for a moment. A group of people has just spent a considerable amount of time concentrating on the disease that afflicts their institution. They spend over a third of their time at work. How much time can a person or group spend discussing irresponsibility, foul language, disrespect, violence, maladjustment, lack of support, and an array of other negative behaviors without beginning to feel somewhat down?

By the time this meeting is over, the staff is probably overwhelmed with a feeling of dread. This was caused, of course, by spending their time dwelling on what is wrong with the school. As is the case in many such situations, much of the staff leaves the meeting fully convinced that nothing can or will be done, the problem is too great, and there is probably no viable solution to these insurmountable problems.

Positive Model for Change

Fortunately, there is another model for creating a school climate wherein things work and morale is high.

The Positive Model For Change (PMFC) can be understood from two perspectives. The first is a perceptual explanation. PMFC incorporates a perceptual shift from a focus on what is missing, wrong, or inappropriate to a view that frames the situation or organization from a "futures" perspective. The shift is from "what is" to "what could be," with an emphasis on what will work, what will be right, and what will benefit all involved.

PMFC can also be interpreted from a behavioral point of view. In this view, the behaviors or actions of the individuals or organizations involved are focused on building successes, strengths, potency, and health. This, of course, is the opposite of attempting to remove inappropriate elements of the system in the hope that their removal will automatically result in their replacement with appropriate components.

The Positive Model for Change begins with a very different set of assumptions than the models that focus on removing negatives. PMFC assumes the following:

- There is more good than bad at this school.

- The entire school community is more comfortable when things are working the way they should.

- The majority of the students will go in the directions they are taken.

- Support is available from outside sources if requested.

- It is less stressful to focus on how the school would look if everyone practiced the habits of good character rather than emphasizing the problems.

- It is easier to build good habits across the institution than it is to eradicate bad habits.

If we look for what "can be," we can overcome what "should not be."

Now, imagine a very different meeting taking place at Bruce Street School. The meeting is opened with the announcement by the principal that the staff will be divided into groups and given markers and newsprint. They are then charged with the task of brainstorming the question, "What would our school and students look like if this were a perfect school?" This exercise, if taken seriously, is structured to generate a composite list very different from the previous meetings.

When finished, some of the statements generated at this meeting might be:

- Students and staff would act respectfully toward each other.

- Students would take their work seriously.

- Parents would be involved in the school.

- There would be "peace in the valley."

- Students would take constructive criticism without getting angry.

- Students and staff would be on time.

- There would be a caring atmosphere at the school.

Once the participants (preferably the entire staff) have created a positive list such as the one above and prioritized the items, the next step would be to decide how to build, reinforce, recognize, and maintain respect, promptness, caring, responsibility, and the other attributes of good character suggested by the list.

Generating a list by going through a process of looking at what "can be" rather than trying to change what "should not be" is a completely different approach to creating change within an institution. By using the positive approach, organizations and institutions can foster creative change. It is also a far less stressful procedure than the burdensome task of focusing on the negative.

Attitudes and Perceptions

Attitudes and perceptions play a critical role in determining how individuals and institutions deal with problematic situations. Anyone who has had the privilege of visiting a variety of schools can attest to the fact that two schools with almost identical demographics can function very differently. One school may be upbeat and positive, wherein the teaching and learning processes flourish. The other school may have an atmosphere of low morale, despair, and unfriendliness wherein teaching and learning barely exist. If the two schools are similar in all objective manners, then to what can the differences be attributed? In most cases, the disparity is the result of collective perceptions and attitudes of the members of the respective school communities.

Assuming that you are in the process of planning, implementing, or maintaining a character education program, the following may be helpful as you work with staff and others. We will be looking at some of the conditions that can influence the success of the character education effort. For the most part, these factors relate to how educators view their students and the school in general, as well as the ability to maintain a work environment that is satisfying and productive.

Positive attitudes and perceptions are the best indicators for success.

Let's look at the students who populate our schools. Previously, we pointed out that there is a general feeling, especially among classroom teachers, that young people are not quite as well behaved or respectful as they once were. As you will recall, the perception of the 831 educators who were surveyed ranked students as respectful, responsible, caring, etc. at 2.6 on a Likert scale of 1 to 5. When administered this survey, they were asked to think about students in general *not* their students or their own children. Their responses painted a rather dismal picture.

On the other hand, when teachers were asked about the students in their classrooms or individuals they know personally, their responses were quite different. When informally questioned, they tended to rate their own students much higher in relation to performing with character. This is understandable. The more we know about a person, the greater the chances we will see positive attributes. That is, of course, if we are looking for good qualities.

Students Watch and Listen

Looking for instances of appropriate behavior is one of the foundation attitudes necessary for a successful approach to character education. A second component is the modeling of good character. It is not enough to tell students to be prompt if adults at school are late.

Experienced educators will testify to the fact that students watch adult behavior, they listen to what is being said, and they remember what adults do and say. Veteran teachers, counselors, and administrators frequently recount stories of something they had said to a student only to find years later that the students remembered the situation and the words.

IN MY EXPERIENCE

B. David Brooks: Following an in-service session at a high school in the El Dorado Union High School District in northern California, I was approached by a teacher. He related to me that he had been stopped in a grocery store by a woman who thanked him for advising her son to become an attorney. At the time of the conversation, he admitted he could not remember this particular student and certainly did not recall ever counseling the student to enter law school.

Later that night, he remembered the student as one of the most talkative students he had ever taught. He then recalled saying to the young man whose mouth never stopped going, "Young man, you talk so much, you ought to be a lawyer." Of course, he did not mean that literally. Nevertheless, the boy later reported to his mother that his favorite teacher thought he should become an attorney.

Students pay attention to what adults are saying and doing. Although they may not show how much they are absorbing, they are watching and listening. If educators lecture against smoking and then light up in a car while pulling out of the school parking lot, students will see that contradictory behavior.

When adults at school model the habits of good character, it enhances the chances that the character education efforts will take hold. Discussing how adults model poor or good character is often overlooked when character education programs are implemented. If a character education program is to flourish, then the adults must examine how they model the traits that are subsequently expected of the students.

Basically, the successful implementation and maintenance of an effective character education program hangs on the willingness of the staff, students, parents, and community to look closely at the modeling being done by adults. Another factor is the willingness to examine the perceptions about students, families, and each other and to openly confront attitudes and perceptions that subvert the character development process.

> Adults must model good character because students are always watching and listening.

The following questions can help to clarify the collective perceptions and attitudes of the stakeholders. Asking the right questions and honestly discussing the conclusions can open the doors to developing positive change in attitude and perception. On the other hand, the answers to these questions may also verify the fact that the right attitudes and perceptions are already there. In that case, the foundation is in place and will ease the implementation process.

- Is the teaching of the principles and skills of good character a responsibility of the school?

- Can character skills be taught?

- Do we, as stakeholders in this school, believe that a school climate emphasizing the teaching of character can make a difference?

- Is character education important enough to infuse it with our other responsibilities and duties?

- Do our students have better character than we believe they have?

- In view of outside influences on the character development of our students can we expect to make a positive change?

- If we pursue a systematic character development program, will there be support from the central office, parents, and the community?

- Can we come to consensus on this matter?

- Can we, as stakeholders, agree on a list of commonly shared values or principles?

- Are our students really at risk to the degree that we need to do more than we already are doing?

- Can we cover enough academic content and still focus on character development?

- Are societal problems so overwhelming that this effort will be of such little value and a waste of time that could be better used for academic instruction?

These are some, not all, of the legitimate questions that have been posed by educators. They reflect a genuine concern regarding the viability of introducing systematic character education into the classroom, school, or district. The questions are a reflection of the kinds of inquiries that will surely come from some of those involved in this effort. The importance of posing these and similar questions is that the exercise will serve as a method for determining the attitudes and perceptions that exists within the school community. Those attitudes and perceptions will affect everyone involved in the character education effort.

There have been volumes written about the effect of one's attitude and perception as they relate to success or failure. This is especially true in the case of character education. If a staff believes that teaching the principles, practices, and processes of good character will work, then positive outcomes can be expected. If the staff has the attitude that students do want to know the rules and will in most cases follow them, the foundation for success is in place. Therefore, an important predictor of the success or failure of character education efforts lies in the determination of the attitudes and perceptions among those participating in the establishment of the program.

CASE STUDY

An assistant principal (who will remain anonymous) in Los Angeles County told me of "Henry," a young man in her school who seemingly had no redeeming qualities. When his name came up, teachers moaned. Teachers checked their roll sheets at the beginning of the semester to see if they had the "bad" boy in any of their classes. He attended a middle school with grades six through eight, and he was in his third year at the school. Much of his three years had been spent sitting on the bench outside of the assistant principal's office.

The eighth-grade students at this school participated in an annual field trip to the ballet. The assistant principal did not relish taking Henry to the ballet with the rest of the class. She knew he would cause serious trouble. Before the group left for the ballet, she warned Henry to behave and informed him that he would be sitting next to her on the bus and at the performance. She was very clear that he was not to leave her side.

During the ballet, the assistant principal heard Henry mumble something. When she finally got him to repeat what she thought she heard, she was shocked. To her surprise, he had commented to himself that the male dancer was doing a pirouette incorrectly. She asked him how he knew that. After considerable prodding, he whispered to her that he studied at a ballet studio every day after school and on the weekends.

Remember, this boy was viewed by the staff and most of his peers as having no redeeming qualities. He was seen as disruptive, a gang member, a troublemaker, and lazy.

The assistant principal received permission from Henry to tell a few of her colleagues about his after-school activities. She told only those she could trust not to spread it around. She knew that his fellow gang members would not look kindly on the fact that Henry was studying ballet.

Some teachers started to talk privately to Henry about this positive aspect of his life. Because of his history of negative behavior, he had never before had positive conversations with teachers. These friendly conversations were new to him.

By virtue of these new interactions with a few of the adults at school, one would hope that Henry would turn his life around and become a model student. This did not happen. He continued his negative behavior patterns. What did happen, however, is that staff who had previously been unable to find good in Henry began to find areas where he was doing okay.

There is a lesson in this story that pertains directly to character education: *What we look for is what we will find*. If school personnel are to build a climate and environment that supports strong character, then the view from the educational establishment must be focused on what works, what is right and the other displays of good character.

By the way, everyone predicted that Henry would drop out of school after the eighth grade. He did not. He managed to make it to graduation and afterwards became a professional ballet dancer. There is no way of knowing for sure, but it is probable that the support Henry received during the end of his middle school career was a major factor in his decision to stay in school and follow his dream.

CHAPTER 3

Planning and the Steering Committee

❝In this democracy, as many stakeholders
as possible must be involved in all aspects
of the community's or school's character
education programs if the expectation is
to raise children of good character.[1]❞

Edward F. DeRoche and Mary M. Williams

The first step in planning a successful character education program,
whether it be in a classroom, school, or district is to make sure that all
stakeholders are involved. This vital first step is often overlooked or
does not take into account all those who need to be informed and
included. Both those who favor character education and those who
do not should be included in the process.

Involve Everyone Early in the Process

The problem with excluding various individuals or groups lies in
the difficulties with complaints and negative actions after the fact.
There are numerous examples of schools and districts planning and
implementing various programs without including all who needed to
know and then having the board of education attacked after the
program is implemented. At the point of implementation, it is very
hard to bring those who dissent on board. Better to have them involved
during the process than attacking after all the work is done.

B. David Brooks: I was hired to consult on the implementation of a character education program at a middle school in Scottsdale, Arizona. My presentation was to be made to a group of about 100 teachers. When I entered the cafeteria where the presentation was to take place, I saw immediately that I was going to have a problem. The podium was placed at the front of the cafeteria and the faculty was clustered at the back. They were seated as far as possible from me as they could and still be in the room. Rather than try to get this hostile group to move toward me I rolled the podium in their direction and commenced my session. It was one of the longest two hours I have ever spent!

When it was over, I pulled a few people aside and asked why there was so much resistance. I was not surprised when they told me that the teachers had not been consulted. Teachers felt that they had a full plate already and could not see how to fit in this new program. To add insult to injury, the central office had added an advisory period to their teaching day. Teachers felt that this was an additional teaching assignment that should have gone through the standard process with the union.

Late in the year, I checked with the school, and, as I would have predicted, the character education program had not been implemented.

Let's look at a district-wide approach to include all stakeholders. The first question, of course, is: "Who are the stakeholders?" It is easy enough to identify school staff, students, and parents as prime stakeholders, but the identification of stakeholders must go further. Often, those who are neglected are persons or groups who, for one reason or another, may be opposed to teaching values or character in the schools. Informing before implementation is one simple, effective way to disarm those who believe, for example, that only math, science, and reading should be taught in school and that building character should be left to the home. There are many reasons why some people do not see the need for a school-based character education program. However, experience supports the reality that many dissenters' doubts disappear once these individuals or groups are brought on board and properly informed.

In a number of cases, the authors of this book have worked with dissenters who eventually evolved into the most ardent supporters.

Several years ago, a small school district on the outskirts of Tucson, Arizona, began the process of implementing a district-wide character education program. The district and each school organized a character education steering committee. Each school's committee was encouraged to include participants from diverse sections of their respective communities

The steering committee must be composed of a broad cross-section of stakeholders.

One attendance area in the district was home to many families whose religious orientation dictated that instruction in values was the responsibility of the church and the family alone. They did not want the school district "meddling" in the area of character education.

The character education steering committee recognized this group as a possible obstacle, so from the beginning, they included this group of parents and community members in the planning of the program. At first, the opposing group was adamant—they did not want the school to teach their children values. To counter their strong opposition, the principal had the foresight to provide the group with samples of the entire classroom curriculum that was going to be used. He told them to take the materials home and to their place of worship. He encouraged the parents to study the material and come back to him with their assessment.

At the next community awareness meeting, the group appeared. Their spokesperson informed the principal and members of the steering committee that they had thoroughly reviewed the material and discovered that they only came up with one or two minor objections. They admitted that they had not been fully aware that character education was, in fact, a means for school teachers to reinforce the basic shared values that they now realized were common to their families, their religious beliefs, and the school community.

Establishing the Steering Committee

Selecting and establishing a steering committee is one of the most critical steps in the process of implementing a successful character education program. It should not be considered a one-person job. Three to five key administrators, coordinators, and leaders should be involved in the process of selecting an inclusive committee. It is imperative that the steering committee be comprised of enough individuals to assure a wide range of personality types and differing points of view. Efforts should be made to include conservatives and liberals, various faith communities, law enforcement representatives, business and professional leaders, and, of course, the various individuals and interest groups who are part of the school or district community. Do not shy away from those who may not agree with the idea of systematic character education. As illustrated in the example above from Arizona, they are needed if the program is to succeed.

Involving individuals and groups who do not support character education is often a way to diffuse their opposition.

The recommended size for this initial steering committee may be twenty to twenty-five individuals. They must be interested, focused on needs of the district, have the time available that they are expected to commit to this effort, and be very reliable and responsible. This is not a discussion group. The character education steering committee is a working group and will require that members "put in their time."

In view of the fact that community leaders, parents, administrators, religious leaders, board members, and others will be included in this group, differing opinions will arise. Remember that this steering committee is the place where conflict can lead to positive results.

Experience with steering committees has shown that the initial meetings will involve the airing of differences and concerns—some of it probably heated. Once this period of initial discussion passes, the group will be able to move on to the demanding tasks of developing a philosophy, creating a belief statement, setting goals and objectives, and establishing programs and implementation strategies.

There is no way to determine when the "dust will settle." Some steering committees can air their differences and get down to business in one or two meetings. Others take a little longer. Nevertheless, this airing of differences is a vital step in the bonding process and enhances the probability of success for the character education effort.

The steering committee will set the philosophy and tone for the entire character education effort.

The commitment to character education and the work the steering committee does will determine either the failure or the success of the entire undertaking.

Nine Essential Elements for Success

The success of any program depends on several essential elements. These factors demonstrate that the steering committee has a shared vision for character education. To help your school or district to create an action plan and establish productive implementation strategies, we have created the Nine Essential Elements for Success. This list can be used as a reminder or become an actual checklist of the components necessary for full and successful implementation of the steering committee's responsibilities.

Collaboration: For a systematic character education program to succeed, all stakeholders must be included and heard.

Commitment: Support for the development and infusion of character education must be both top down *and* bottom up. It should not only include an intellectual commitment but also a commitment of resources.

Clarity: There must be a clear understanding of the mission, goals, and objectives of the program. The purpose of character education and the strategies for successful implementation must be explicit, and they must be communicated effectively to all involved.

Comprehensiveness: Character education is comprehensive. It is not a course that students have in the second semester during the fifth period. A successful character education program is infused into the entire curriculum. It also extends throughout the school into all areas of adult-student contact, including clubs, sports, other extracurricular activities, and the overall school climate.

Coherence: The same language must be used in all components of the program. Lesson plans, guidance services, extracurricular activities, and school climate efforts must use the same set of principles, practices, and processes.

Coordination: Character education is a school-wide or district-wide effort. There must be a coordinating person or group to ensure that implementation proceeds according to plan, support is provided, and assessment is carried out.

Competency: Assessment is vital to the ongoing success of the character education program. It is essential to evaluate the degree to which students are acquiring the cognitive and affective competencies that foster the growth of good character habits.

Connections: The principles of good character must be connected to the existing curriculum and activities of the school.

Celebration: Time must be set aside to reflect back on the process and to celebrate the program's successes.

Defining Committee Members' Responsibilities

Although there are many issues that must be discussed from time to time, the character education steering committee is a working committee, not a discussion group. It is task-oriented. As such, it must clearly define the responsibilities and jobs of each member from the beginning. In committing to participate as a member of the steering committee, each person should agree to the following:

- Make a time commitment. Each member will need to commit to attending meetings and completing other tasks and assignments outside of the scheduled meetings.

- Assist in the development and dissemination to all stakeholders of the belief or mission statements related to character education.

- Help develop a philosophy that will clearly define the path upon which this effort will proceed.

- Establish specific goals and objectives for successful implementation.

- Be willing to represent and report to their various constituencies.

- Convey the concerns and recommendations of their constituents to the steering committee.

- Complete comprehensive material/program reviews.

- Determine if a published character education program will be used or if the school/district will create its own curriculum materials. If a published curriculum is to be used, select the program.

- Recommend program material/curriculum to the appropriate division or personnel.

- Support the consensus decisions of the steering committee.

- Establish a timeline for implementation.

- Create or acquire appropriate evaluation instruments.

- Recommend a budget for implementation and ongoing support.

Committee members must be task-oriented "doers" who are committed to seeing their efforts through to completion.

For example, one task of the steering committee members may be to search for an appropriate character education program or curriculum for the school or district. In this capacity, they must be willing to discuss issues and concerns, listen attentively to program representatives, research, explore, and then make recommendations based on a sound rationale, which includes budget considerations.

The steering committee can work as one large unit led by a chairperson. Alternatively, the committee can function in differentiated teams designed to cover more miles in a shorter period. Of course, if the team approach is utilized, there is still the need for full steering committee meetings for the purpose of reviewing, revising, and adopting subcommittee recommendations.

Setting Specific Program Goals

Assuming that a viable committee is in place, it is now time to establish specific goals and incorporate them into a strategic plan. The history of new program implementation within the educational establishment is replete with examples of innovative approaches being implemented without a strategic plan. One of the difficulties of the education profession is that each year the school seems to start all over again from ground zero. The newest trend or approach is often foisted on the classroom teacher only to be discarded once the classroom door is closed.

A closer look at this phenomenon indicates that many times new ideas and the newest strategies are not accompanied by a viable strategic plan. If there is to be effective long-term implementation of new or improved approaches to educating students, there must be a specific plan for implementation, support, adjustment, and evaluation.

In My Experience

B. David Brooks: As a principal at John Glenn High School in Norwalk, California, I once took the time to go through classrooms during the summer. I looked in closets and cabinets and, to my dismay, found thousands and thousand of dollars worth of curriculum materials that had never even been opened. Much of it was material associated with some "new trend" that had come and gone.

Setting goals is a primary function of the steering committee. Obviously, it is very important that all the stakeholders are involved in the goal-setting process. The steering committee is generally a recommending body. Recommendations, of course, require final approval by those who must lend both moral and financial support. It would be useless to set goals that were not supported by the superintendent and the board.

There are many formats for setting goals. Some are very complicated and include the goal, objectives, strategies, and elaborate assessment procedures. We recommend that the goal-setting procedure be kept as simple as possible. Do not get bogged down in the process. The members of the committee have many other commitments. The steering committee will need to be careful or the planning process will become another full-time job for the members.

> One of the first tasks is to set goals for both the committee and the character education program.

At its best, creating and establishing goals can be a trying process. It is helpful to follow some simple guidelines when drafting the goals. By considering each of the guidelines suggested below, the steering committee can stay focussed and hopefully avoid the time-consuming delays that can come from discussions (a.k.a. arguments) about specific wording. Keep it simple.

Minimally, each goal should include the following components:

- what is going to be accomplished

- when it is going to be accomplished

- how it is to be evaluated

- who is responsible for accomplishing it

Examine this sample goal:

> Goal III: The steering committee will pre-test all staff, using the Character Education Staff Survey. The Character Education Staff Survey will be administered during the opening of the school staff development day 8/27/02. The completed surveys will be collected during the staff development day and be turned over to the district testing and evaluation office for analysis. The analysis will be presented to the Steering Committee by 9/1/02. Committee members John McCulloch and Samantha Carter will be responsible for this goal.

What is going to be accomplished? The steering committee will pre-test all staff using the Character Education Staff Survey.

When will the administration of the survey be accomplished? The Character Education Staff Survey will be administered during the opening of the school staff development day 8/27/02.

How will this survey be evaluated? The completed surveys will be collected during the staff development day and be turned over to the district testing and evaluation office for analysis. The analysis will be presented to the Steering Committee by 9/1/02.

Who is responsible for the survey? Committee members John McCulloch and Samantha Carter will be responsible this goal.

Yes, the goal appears somewhat lengthy, but it leaves no doubt as to the process. The language is very simple and direct. If you prepare your character education goals following this template (or one like it), you can help move the goal-setting process forward in a timely manner and avoid delays by any "wordsmiths" on the steering committee.

Categories of Goals

Minimally, the list of goals developed by the steering committee should cover these areas:

Mission or Vision Statement: The committee must establish a goal for an inclusive process to develop a mission or vision statement that can be accepted by all the stakeholders. This is generally the first goal of the committee, and, once accomplished, it will provide the foundation for setting additional goals.

Timeline: The committee must examine their overall schedule and accept that the process of establishing a school- or district-wide character education program will take time. Most importantly, full implementation will not occur in one school year. The schedule should be realistic and take into account that this process is multiyear. The goal of setting a timeline should be the second step. The committee will want to look at all their implementation goals and relate them to the timeline.

Program Components: A goal to examine existing curriculums and strategies, as well as other methods for evaluating classroom and school climate should be included. Many long-term decisions of the committee will be based on the results of this goal. This goal sets the stage for determining whether a published curriculum will be used or if the school or district will devise lessons and activities internally. A combination of several approaches may also be used to implement character education.

Strategic Plan: In order to move character from the invisible to the visible (back burner to the front burner), it is necessary that a goal be established that addresses the inclusion of character education as one of the elements of the district's and the schools' strategic plans. By placing character education into the strategic plans, the probability for success increases substantially.

Cost Analysis and Budgets: The implementation of a systematic character education program will cost money. There will be a need for staff development, the purchase of a curriculum or time for staff to develop one themselves, printing, and other communication costs. The question as to the source of funds must be answered. If grants are to be submitted, then one of the goals under this category should reflect how and when this important task will be accomplished. Additionally, another goal in this category should include the projected or actual budget for full implementation (See Appendix F).

Evaluation: This goal is vital. Often programs are established without an evaluation component. When this happens, the chances for success are significantly diminished. Setting a goal for ongoing evaluation ensures that mid-course corrections can be made and successes can be reported. This goal helps the school or district know if they are moving in the planned direction.

As mentioned above, these are the minimal goal requirements for the steering committee. Nevertheless, the steering committee may want to consider other goals such as including the community, communicating with those inside and outside of the school, revision of policies, and the establishment of subcommittees or working groups to compete tasks outside of the purview of the steering committee. It is important that the goals of the steering committee are clear and that they are communicated to all that will have a part in this important process.

> The steering committee must be sure that their goals cover all aspects of the program and that they are attainable.

There is an additional admonition that is vital at this point. To put it simply, the steering committee members must do their homework before they set their goals. If money is to be expended, someone on the committee must communicate with the holder(s) of the purse strings. The committee must determine if the money is available, when it will be available, how much will be available, and how it can be spent. It may seem terribly obvious, but many programs have stalled because the steering committees didn't bring the "funding stakeholders" into the goal-setting process. To plan for staff development and the purchase of curriculum materials without the input and approval of those responsible for funds will only lead to frustration and failure.

The Importance of Communication

Throughout all the stages of your character education program—planning, implementation, and evaluation—nothing is more important than clear, complete, honest, and frequent communication. Communication must occur among the members of the steering committee, with the administration, with the board, with staff, with parents and students, and with the community at large.

During the early phases of planning and goal-setting, good communication can mean the difference between success and total failure. Communication with different interest groups and stakeholders can take different forms—newsletters to parents, meeting minutes to administrators, and memos to staff. No matter how the steering committee chooses to communicate, at least one person should have the responsibility of being the liaison between the steering committee and the district administration or board of education.

Imagine a situation where a steering committee has been working diligently to start a systematic character education program. One of their goals is to have the board pass a resolution designed to support the character education effort. However, no member of the committee has communicated with the administration to determine whether the board will approve such a resolution. The resolution is presented to the board for a vote. Because it hasn't been kept in the loop, the board does not pass the resolution, and no funding can be directed to the planned character education program. The phrase "dead in the water" comes to mind!

Good communication is key to program success.

The scenario above is not far-fetched, nor is it atypical, unfortunately. It happens all the time, and it underscores the need for clear communication between the steering committee and all stakeholders. Communication doesn't just mean disseminating information, it also means receiving and listening to feedback.

In their book *Educating Heart and Minds*, DeRoche and Williams stress the importance effective communication. They state:

> . . . other people in and out of the daily operation of the program need to know what's going on and why. In planning and implementing character education programs in a language that the community understands, the mission and the expectations, and he styles and methods of delivery, are very important. The purpose of effective external communication is to build confidence, engender support, and encourage participation in the work of the [steering committee]. Therefore, some of the following conditions for effective communication require attention.
>
> Policy: Does the [steering committee] have a written policy about its communication efforts that addresses both internal and public matters?
>
> Roles: Do group members know their roles? Do they know who is to do what and when they are to do it? Is it clear to each member what he or she can and should say as a [steering committee] member and as a private party?
>
> Specialists: Does the [steering committee] use the experts in their community—media people, marketing and promotion specialists, university researchers, companies whose work it is to poll the pubic—to help communicate with the public and particularly with parents? Because communication is a two-way process, these groups can help the [steering committee] "hear" what the public is saying about their efforts and the programs being implemented.
>
> Barriers: Does the [steering committee] attend to potential communication barriers? One obvious barrier can be the language of the people. Communication efforts must address the various languages that people speak in their homes and neighborhoods. Other barriers requiring attention include biases, prejudices, special interest groups, traditions, cultural heritages, and ways to deliver information.

Plans: Does the [steering committee] have well-developed communication plans? Are there plans for distribution of meeting minutes, for public bulletins, for inter-group communication, for newsletters, for events calendars, and for celebrations? Do the plans include ways for getting feedback from community groups, from parents and students, from critics and supporters, from leaders and participants?[2]

The implementation of a systematic character program will have detractors and supporters. The character education steering committee has the responsibility and the opportunity to conduct itself in a manner that will diminish opposition and reinforce and increase support. Clear goals along with open and effective communications are the tools to use in moving character education forward.

CASE STUDY

During the 1995–96 school year, the Humble Independent School District (Humble, Texas) established a steering committee and followed similar guidelines to those presented in this chapter to determine a timeline, a belief statement, goals, and a list of core principles.

The steering committee was composed of a broad cross section of school and community stakeholders:

- Assistant Superintendent, Curriculum
- Community religious leader
- Corporate executive
- Director of Curriculum and Instruction
- Director of the Lake Houston YMCA
- Evaluation and Assessment Coordinator
- First grade parent
- K–12 Language Arts Coordinator
- Kindergarten parent
- Lakeland Elementary principal

- Lakeland Elementary school counselor
- PTA president
- School Psychologists Program Director
- Science Coordinator
- Special Populations Coordinator
- Special Services Director
- Student Wellness Coordinator
- Two Humble ISD school board members
- Woodland Hills Elementary principal

As a result of the work of the committee, the following documents were presented to the administration and board and approved for district-wide dissemination.

Humble Independent School District
Character Education
Belief Statement

- That our students are best taught by example. Whether our role is as a parent, teacher, administrator, coach, bus driver, cafeteria staff member, or as a community member, our Character Development Program will be effective only if we model it in our daily lives;

- That each student, staff member, and parent holds an individual belief system that is bound by specific religious, cultural, and governmental parameters that must be respected;

- That there are fundamental principles that must be taught in order to perpetuate a democratic society.

District Goals

I. All district personnel will respect students, as well as expect students to respect them.

II. All district personnel will model behavior reflective of Humble ISD's six core principles and will expect students to display these same behaviors.

III. The Humble ISD Character Development Program will reinforce and promote good citizenship.

IV. Parents and community members will participate in and support the Humble ISD Character Development Program.

V. The Six Pillars of Character will be embedded into all curricular areas, as well as all school-based programs and activities.

Humble Independent School District
Committed to Character Development

- Publicly supports the Six Pillars of Character

- Defines those traits in terms of observable behavior

- Models those traits at every opportunity

- Studies them and teaches their application to real-life situations

- Holds all school members accountable to standards of conduct

CHAPTER 4

Assessing Your School's "Character Climate"

❝To me, character education is a very important component of a school system. I don't see a school as just an academic facility; it's also a place where students can learn to develop and cultivate their character. Thus, more students can become good and productive members of any community they choose to join.[1]❞

Michael Hurley, high school student

As discussed in Chapter 1, character education is the systematic, purposeful teaching of core consensus values that leads to habits of good character. It also focuses on:

- cooperative relationships and mutual respect

- the capacity to think, feel, and act morally

- making informed decisions

Effective character education based on the Three P's (*principals*, *practice*, and *process*) results in a school climate based on fairness, caring, and participation, mutual respect, and responsibility.

As one looks at schools, it is obvious that each school has an institutional culture. This is true of schools at all grade levels. In some schools, the culture or climate is upbeat, productive, and leads to an

Each school has an institutional culture that is reflected in the behaviors of the individuals and groups within the school community.

environment where teaching and learning are paramount. On the opposite end of the normal curve, there are schools where the climate borders on depression. It is a simple fact that each school evolves its unique climate because of the interactions of staff and students. A school where systematic character education is in place will have a climate conducive to learning and teaching.

It is important to keep in mind that character education is as important in high school as it is in the lower grades. At times, high schools are viewed more from an academic or curricular perspective, with less emphasis on the individual social, personal, and emotional needs of students. While character education at the high school level may be approached differently than at lower grade levels, it is still a vital part of the educational experience.

Identify the Stakeholders

If there is to be an assessment of the climate of a school in relation to character education, it is important to determine who and what it is that will be appraised. The first step, of course, is to define who the stakeholders are. Obviously, major stakeholders are the students, teachers, and administrators. What is not so obvious are the "invisible " teachers. Generally, we think of classroom teachers as the core of the instructional program at a school. This is true; teachers are the main purveyors of educational content. However, all education in a school, especially character education, is not derived only from classroom instruction. Much of what students learn comes from their interpretations of the modeling of *all adults* at the school.

For example, when a student sees an adult smoking, she does not ask herself if the smoker has a teaching credential. She views the smoker as an adult and interprets the modeling of smoking behavior positively or negatively, depending on what she knows about smoking and her relationship with that particular person. Perhaps the smoker is the school secretary for whom the student has considerable respect. If that is the case, the student may view smoking as an acceptable behavior. The school secretary, therefore, becomes a "invisible teacher" and a stakeholder in the character education process.

All stakeholders must be involved from the beginning of the implementation process. The list of stakeholders may vary depending on the willingness to involve special interest groups or others. The rule of thumb should be "more is better." Some, not all, of those who should be considered as important members of a comprehensive character education efforts are:

- certified staff
- non-certified or classified staff
- students
- substitute teachers
- bus drivers and crossing guards
- board members
- political leaders
- clergy (all faiths)
- law enforcement agencies
- parents
- the Chamber of Commerce and other business groups
- professional organizations
- social service agencies
- youth-serving organizations
- the justice system
- community-based services and agencies
- others who have an interest in the wellness of the schools and community

The effective implementation of a character education program depends, to a great degree, on educating stakeholders prior to implementation. That is, all of the school community must be aware of the plan for moving forward. The process of informing or educating the stakeholders should focus on the school's philosophy. Consideration should also be given to:

- the composition of the student body

- the demographics of the community

- the goals and expectations of the staff

- the goals and expectations of parents

- the concerns of all members of the school or district community

Implementation without educating the stakeholders will forestall progress.

Assessing Attitudes

In the assessment process, some essential questions must be asked about the current awareness of the staff, students, and others as related to systematic character education. What is the level of understanding? Is there a total lack of awareness, some knowledge, or considerable understanding of the issues related to character education?

Before actually assessing attitudes and knowledge, the school or district should create the character education steering committee. As we discussed in the previous chapter, the character education steering committee needs to be a stand-alone entity; it can not be a subcommittee of another unit. If character education is to be seen as a high priority, status must be given to this body. Secondly, the character education steering committee must be inclusive. The most effective committee will include representative of all the factions within the school community.

Once a viable steering committee is established, their first task should be assessment. At this early stage of implementation, the assessment should be primarily focused on three steps. The first step is to determine what currently exists in the schools and classrooms that supports the systematic teaching of the *principles*, *practice*, and *process* (the Three P's) of good character. It should be understood that educators teach and model good (or poor) character every day. This assessment is not focused at that level. This assessment will look for specific curriculum, activities, programs, and other strategies that are being used currently to teach the principles and practices of good character.

The second step of the assessment processes it to determine how the adults view students in relation to their practicing good character. This is a perceptual assessment. It is important to know if the adults who interact with students perceive students as having a high, medium, or low level of character traits such as honesty, respect, caring, responsibility, etc. This assessment is important because it will give an overall picture of adult perceptions. If, for example, the educators perceive their students as dishonest, disrespectful and irresponsible, it can lead to actions that actually reinforce the inappropriate behaviors of students.

> Perceptions shape the view one has of the world and can lead to actions that support that view.

Perceptions are important because they help shape the way we interact with others. The Character Education Survey (Appendix A) has been used as a pre- and post-survey to assess the perceptions of staff. Comparisons of pre- and post-surveys demonstrate that the implementation of a systematic character education program results in a positive shift in perceptions. The two statements shown in the figure below are typical pre- and post-survey responses.

Average Perceptions on Pre and Post Surveys
Five-point scale: 1 strongly disagree – 5 strongly agree.

	Before Character Education	After Character Education
Students are trustworthy.	2.5	3.0
Teachers can trust students to be responsible.	2.0	3.0
Cheating is rare at this school.	1.3	2.4
Students display caring behavior toward staff.	2.4	3.1
Students react respectfully when disciplined.	1.5	2.0
Students are aware of the steps to be taken when resolving problems.	1.5	3.5

These average scores, taken from a survey at a middle school in central Louisiana, demonstrate that the perceptions of staff shifted toward the positive after one year of systematic character education. The importance of this shift, combined with anecdotal reports from staff at the school, supported the conclusion that the change in the way students were viewed by the staff was accompanied by changes in their interactions with students, i.e. they more frequently recognized and reinforced positive behaviors in their students. In addition, there was a positive shift in staff morale.

A steering committee may, of course, want to develop an assessment tailored to specific needs. Some of the questions that have been included in individual assessments include:

• What is the perceived level of student trustworthiness?

• Is there a cheating problem at the school?

• How do students handle responsibility?

• Are students responsible about turning in assignments on time?

• Would it be obvious to an outside observer that the school is a caring, nurturing environment?

- Is there a high or low degree of mutual respect between students and adults?

- Do students use appropriate language?

- Is fairness generally seen as an integral part of the interactions between members of the school community?

- What is the level of community service performed by students?

- Do students understand that their choices result in consequences?

- Are students equipped to make reasonable decisions, plan for the future, and resolve conflicts peacefully?

- Is there a conflict resolution model used by students and staff?

One other important area of assessment centers on the students' ability to define and/or describe examples of caring, trustworthiness, respect, etc. The Student Character Education Survey (Appendix B) has been used as a pre- and post-assessment of students' awareness of the behaviors or actions related to good and poor character.

While it is not enough that students can articulate the appropriate character actions, it is an important first step in forming the habits of good character. This type of student survey provides staff with information about the level of knowledge students have. It can also be used to determine whether or not students can identify appropriate behavior. Experience with this survey indicates that the introduction of systematic character education leads to an increase in knowledge of what constitutes both good and poor character. The assumption can be made that an increase in the knowledge about what constitutes a trustworthy person, for example, can lead to the ability to make more informed decisions, thereby leading to good character practices.

IN MY EXPERIENCE

B. David Brooks: At Emperor Elementary School in San Gabriel, California, the character emphasis is language. Each year, the school focuses on a single theme. The theme is defined and integrated into the curriculum at the beginning of the school year. As a beginning activity, students are asked to write about the theme. This is the first step in creating the knowledge base for understanding the theme or principle.

For example, in 1999–2000, the yearly principle was *perseverance*, and students were instructed to write about the following: Have you ever been in situation where you had to show initiative and not give up?

This writing exercise began the process for students of assimilating the principle. It helped them form the knowledge base necessary for translating the principle, perseverance, into practice.

To further this language acquisition process, Emperor Elementary School, whose mascot is an eagle, developed the "I's" code of conduct.

EAGLE "I'S"

I will respect others' rights.
Keep hands, feet, and all objects to myself.

I will be a respectful listener.
Respect others' opinions.

I will be a responsible person.
Complete all work and make good choices.

I will make wise decisions.
Consider others' feelings as well as my own.

I will work for the best solution.
Develop a positive attitude that all things can be worked out.

Did the increase of knowledge of the principles of good character have an effect on the behavior of students at Emperor? According to Kathy Perini, the principal, there has been a dramatic decline in disciplinary referrals to the office. During the 1993–1994 school year, during which the Emperor character education program was launched, there were 105 referrals for disciplinary infractions. During the 1998–1999 school year, there were only 31 referrals, a drop of 70 percent.

Assess Student Behaviors

Finally, the steering committee will want to obtain hard data related to student behavior. This data should include information related to discipline referrals, truancy, tardiness, and other disciplinary actions. This is valuable because it is benchmark information that can be compared with information following implementation of the character education program.

For example, at Kingwood Middle School in Kingwood, Texas, Mr. Doug Monk, the assistant principal, compiled information from the first quarter of the year prior to implementation of school-wide character education. The following year after the first nine weeks of character education at the school, he compare the data from the previous year to data from the first nine weeks of the implementation year. The results demonstrated that the introduction of character education—the only major change in the operation of the school—was having a positive effect on student behavior. Some of the results are shown in the table below.

Student Behaviors	1998	1999	% change
Students receiving five or more demerits	98	71	− 28%
Students issued school service for disciplinary infractions	125	60	− 52%
Students issued detentions	106	57	− 46%
Students issued Saturday detentions	84	66	− 21%
Students issued alternative class assignments	27	10	− 63%

The accumulation of data from the pre-implementation year allowed Mr. Monk and the staff to assess progress at his school.

A Character Skills Survey

There are a variety of ways to assess the perceptions of adults regarding the character of the students in the school or district. One of the most efficient ways is to have staff members complete a questionnaire or survey. In order to obtain quantitative data, the survey should be set up for respondents to express their opinions on a scale that allows them to indicate the degree or strength of their opinions. A five-, seven-, or ten-point scale is often used, with one end of the scale indicating strong agreement with a statement and the other end indicating strong disagreement.

Some surveys may also include items that require a written response from respondents. While the information provided may provide insight into certain beliefs, situations, or attitudes, this type of data is often difficult to quantify.

One assessment tool that is readily available to you is the Character Education Survey found in Appendix A at the end of this book. This forty-question survey uses a one-to-five Likert scale, with "one" indicating strong agreement and "five" indicating strong disagreement. This tool has been used successfully by a variety of school districts and has provided valuable quantitative data.

Prior to implementation, the survey can be used to assess staff attitudes and perceptions. This information can help shape the overall character education program's goals and strategies for achieving those goals. The survey should be administered again at the end of the school year or at predetermined milestones to help evaluate the effectiveness of the overall program.

Assessment does not stop at the end of this planning stage. Assessment needs to be an ongoing component of the character education effort. Huffman[2] writes: "Implementation assessment is often overlooked, and yet poor implementation of a program is frequently the cause of disappointing results. A careful assessment of the implementation process can reveal a variety of problems that can be corrected through mid-course adjustments." He continues, "Sometimes, a vital component will have been omitted in the planning process. In other situations, staff development for some aspect of a program has been insufficient."

Just as we have learned to evaluate student progress through a variety of ongoing assessments, we must also use ongoing assessment to evaluate the program's effectiveness. The analyzed data can provide important information about ways in which the program has succeeded and areas that need improvement.

CASE STUDY

B. David Brooks recalls: When I was a counselor at a high school in Norwalk, California, I was asked by the district assistant superintendent how I thought my colleagues viewed their students and how that might affect adult and student relationships. The student population was about 1,500 students, and there was heavy gang involvement.

I told the assistant superintendent that I was not sure and that I would conduct a formal assessment. My less-than-scientific study consisted of two elements. First, I simply asked staff members what they thought about the students at the school. In the second part of my "investigation," I observed the teachers and compared their stated feelings about students with their actual interactions with them.

The majority of the teachers and staff I questioned felt students were disrespectful and irresponsible. In addition, a small number of the persons I talked with were actually afraid of their students.

Having determined the prevailing attitudes, I watched the interactions. Almost all of those who had the opinion that students were disrespectful or irresponsible treated their students with disrespect. Not only were these teachers less than respectful, in several cases, they failed to follow through with things they said they would do. For example, a number of students told me that they were always in trouble for being late to class even though the teachers who disciplined them were often late themselves.

On the other hand, teachers who viewed their students much more positively appeared more friendly, involved, and helpful toward students.

When I compared the number of disciplinary referrals to the office generated by the two groups, I was not surprised to find that the teachers who viewed students in a more positive light had significantly fewer referrals.

As I said, this was not a strict scientific study, but my observations were enough to convince me that the manner in which we perceive individuals or groups affects how we treat them.

If my informal analysis were to be applied to a character education program, it would indicate that we should provide some sort of training to the staff that helped them realize that their attitudes and behaviors have a strong effect on students' attitudes and behaviors.

CHAPTER 5

Language, Principles, and Practice

"Our schools, for the most part, do a wonderful job. From first grade through graduate school, they offer a multitude of courses that result in increased knowledge and valuable skills. But something is missing from the curriculum. We don't teach our students about life itself, about how it works, or about what is essential. Never has there been a greater need.[1]"

Hal Urban

In the previous chapters, we have defined character education and have provided reasons for upgrading the teaching and modeling of good character in classrooms and schools. In this chapter, we will examine the "languaging" process and how it contributes to the development of character. By "languaging," we mean the process by which individuals use language to receive and interpret linguistic input, think, communicate, and make ethical decisions. Additionally, we will present the first two of the three elements necessary for establishing a powerful character education program.

Stages of Language Acquisition and Use

The acquisition of language and its uses are complex. However, there are some fundamental ideas about language that can contribute to the establishment of a climate for good character in a classroom or school.

Consequently, we will discuss language and the languaging process from a common sense point of view rather than a scientific or linguist's perspective.

For the purpose of this discussion, "language" includes:

- the words we say to each other

- the words and thoughts we have in our own minds

- feelings and emotions

- the pictures we see

- the sounds we hear

- the games we play

- the lessons we learn

- the accumulation or combination of all of the above

Think of language acquisition and use as having four stages. These stages are not definitive. That is, we cannot say with any certainty when an individual moves from one stage to the next. Nevertheless, consideration of these stages can help us structure a character education program in a way that will increase the probability of success.

An individual starts life in the first stage with no verbal language other than random sounds. As the child begins to develop words, he or she enters the second stage, what we will call "childhood language." Childhood language has certain characteristics. Young children are very self-centered in their language. Words like *me* and *mine* are common. As the child matures, of course, his or her language changes as he or she becomes socialized at home and in school.

The third stage is a transitional phase. It is the period when the individual is moving from childlike thinking to a more adult way of processing words and symbols. During this stage, individuals gain an increased ability to interpret input. Finally, in the fourth stage, the adult phase, there is much more interpretation, synthesis, and integration taking place. Language and the processing of input are treated in a much more sophisticated and complex manner. Simply put, as children grow into adults, they mature in their thinking and languaging abilities.

Literal Language and Thinking

This languaging concept is related to character education in a couple of ways. The first is to understand that the childlike thinkers are more literal than logical, whether they are five, fifteen, or fifty-five. This has important implications when we are helping students, especially literal-thinking students, to acquire specific character related behaviors.

> Language development and acquisition has a strong impact on a person's thinking process.

We always need to assume that most students are literal thinkers. They accept what is being said at face value. They do not translate or interpret "what is said" into "what is meant." Literal thinkers take things literally. For example, a teacher wants her students to walk in line with their hands at their sides. The reason she wants her children to walk with their hands at their sides is that she does not want any pushing or shoving. Not taking into consideration that many of her students are literal thinkers, she says, "As we go down the hall, I want you to walk in line. Do not to touch the person in front of you or behind you." Halfway down the hall, she notices that two boys are walking with their arms extended as though they were airplanes and a third is clapping his hands over his head. Consequently, the three get into trouble for not walking with their arms at their sides.

Were they told to walk with their arms at their sides? No. They were told something very different and did not have the maturity or ability to translate the instructions into "keep your arms at your sides."

Character education is about teaching children to practice the behaviors that will lead to the formation of the habits of good character. When we fail to recognize that students tend to interpret language literally, then we are making the job of encouraging the habits of good character much more difficult. We can never assumed that students will translate "don't touch the person in front of you or behind you" into "I'm supposed to keep my hands at my sides."

The implication for character education, especially with younger children, is to tell the students what is expected. In *Lessons In Character*,[2] there is a poster in the form of a calendar with the days of the week. Across the top of the poster are six character traits and a decision-making model. Each day has a different way in which kindergarten children can display good character. All of the desired behaviors are presented in a positive manner that literal-thinking kindergartners can understand. For example:

Trustworthiness:	Tell the Truth and Return What You Borrow
Respect:	Be Polite and Use Courteous Words
Responsibility:	Do Your Own Work and Keep Trying
Fairness:	Listen to Others and Take Only Your Share
Caring:	Be Helpful and Say Something Kind
Citizenship:	Follow Rules and Care for the Environment
S.T.A.R.:	Stop Before You Act and Think Before You Act

With language used in this manner, there is little room for guessing. Effective character education programs must strive to keep the language clear so students are aware of the expectations and the consequences.

Using direct, literal language to communicate expectations and consequences can help lead students toward developing the habits of good character. However, it is not the only way that language can contribute to the character education effort.

At Cotswold Elementary School (K–5), in Charlotte, North Carolina, principal Donna Cianfrani and her staff instituted a language approach in an effort to foster good character. They agreed to address the students by saying, "please," "thank you," and "you are welcome." In addition, the staff spoke to students who were misbehaving by first asking them, "Are you doing the right thing?"

These approaches may seem simplistic. In reality, they are not. This use of pro-character language leads to an increase in awareness on the part of students (and adults) and ultimately to the formation of the habits of good character. When students hear polite language, they will tend to imitate that language.

Taking the language approach one step further, the students and staff created the Cotswold Character Pledge, which is recited each day after the Pledge of Allegiance.

> The use of spoken and printed language can have a strong effect on the success of a character education program.

THE COTSWOLD CHARACTER PLEDGE

I believe that I can be a good student.
I believe I can show good character.
I believe that when I work hard I will succeed.
So, I will work hard each day to do my best.
I can learn. I will learn.

In My Experience

B. David Brooks: I had just completed a staff development session for the Los Angeles Unified School District when a teacher approached me. She started the conversation by telling he how important words are and how they can have a lasting effect on students.

She went on to relate how her parents moved during the first semester of her senior year. Having spent her entire school career in the same school district, moving to a new school was devastating to her. At the new school where she knew no one, she was very lonely and homesick for her former classmates.

On the second day at the new school, she was called to the principal's office. When she arrived, the principal had her school records on his desk and began the conversation by welcoming her to the school.

She told me that this was the only time she talked to the principal, and she could not remember his name or what he looked like. Nevertheless, she clearly remembered his words.

During the conversation, the principal asked her what she planned to do after graduation. She responded that she would probably get married and have a family. Women from her cultural background were not encouraged to continue their educations. The principal asked her if she had ever thought about going to college and perhaps becoming a teacher. "No," she replied. "No one in my family has ever graduated from high school. I am the first one. I've never thought about going to college or becoming a teacher." They talked a little longer and the principal continued to encourage her to consider college.

She told me that when she left the office, she knew the seed was sown. After a little heavy-duty persuasion with her family, especially her father, she received permission to go to college after high school. When I spoke with her, she was a fourth grade teacher in Los Angeles.

I took note of the fact that she did not remember the principal's name or even what he looked like, but she clearly remembered his words. I asked her if I could tell her story to the others at the session because it so clearly demonstrated how important words can be. She gave me permission, and

I asked her the name of the school and the year she graduated. She told me the school was John Glenn High School in Norwalk, California, and the year was 1979.

I was amazed because *I* was the principal of John Glenn high School in 1979. I did not remember her either, but I always called new students into my office to welcome them.

We must always be careful of what we say. We never know what words our students take away with them.

The Three P's

Effective character education should be composed of three essential elements. They are the "Three P's." The first P constitutes the **principles** around which the program is built. The second P represents the **practice** of the skills, attitudes, actions, and habits of good character. The third P stands for the **process** by which an organization, group, or individual makes decisions, resolves conflicts, or sets goals.

Educators can best structure their character education effort if the Three P's are central elements of the language and culture at school. Principles, practice, and process must become part of the language, attitudes, expectations, and behaviors of all of the members of the school community.

Think about some of the words and phrases that are so effectively used by the advertising industry:

Free	Price Reduction	Sale
One of a Kind	New and Improved	Last Chance
No Interest	Free Shipping	Act Today

These words are used repeatedly for a reason. Over long periods of time and extensive exposures, words like the ones above have been proved to catch the attention of potential customers. The words have become part of the thinking process—the languaging—of the individual.

Think of that wonderful office and household product that we cannot do without—we use it to stick things on the wall, wrap packages, repair torn currency. We call it Scotch tape. It really is not Scotch® tape. Actually, it is cellophane tape but we call it Scotch tape because those words have become embedded in our thinking (much to the joy of 3M, the makers of Scotch® brand cellophane tape).

How many of these do you know?

> LSMFT _____
>
> You'll wonder where the _____ went.
>
> It's a small world _____.
>
> Just for the taste of it, diet _____!
>
> It takes two hands to handle a _____.
>
> _____, where quality is job 1!
>
> Chevy trucks. Like a _____!
>
> Yo quiero _____ _____.
>
> _____ is ready when you are.

Corporations spend millions of dollars on advertising their products. They employ visual and oral advertisements. They have the "beautiful people" model the commodity. They make sure the brand name goes into the potential customer's eyes, ears, and, hopefully, minds. There is only one reason for the expenditure of time, talent, and money. The marketing and advertising agencies want the consumer to acquire brand recognition and then translate that knowledge into a positive attitude about the produce or service.

The advertising industry knows that presentation of the language and the formation of a positive attitude or perception will lead to buying behavior. If they achieve the goal of having shoppers know and feel good about the product, then the odds are favorable that the consumer will make a purchase.

Language and the languaging process become a constant part of our consciousness when we are surrounded (or in the case of advertising, bombarded) with it.

Principles

Words, images, and all the other components of language are important and can change the way organizations, institutions, groups, and/or individuals view themselves or how others view them. For example, Auburn University officials have decided to give their football stadium a nickname. The university, whose mascot is a tiger, is calling Jordan-Hare Stadium "The Jungle." The reasoning behind this is the hope that the nickname will add excitement for the fans and strike fear into the hearts of their opponents. Isn't this a little silly? Not according to the people who are spending a lot of money to create a jungle atmosphere within the stadium and the merchandizing company that will produce and sell cups, hats, T-shirts, and other souvenirs touting the idea that to play Auburn, you must go into their jungle. They know that this kind of language manipulation works.

It also works with the presentation of the principles of good character. If students are expected to develop the habits of good character, then they need to be familiar with the principles upon which the practices of good character are based. Students need to know the "value" words such as responsibility, respect, caring, and trustworthiness.

It is clear that there are basic principles or values that bind a society. Although these are commonly held core consensus values, different groups, communities, organizations, or schools may choose to use slightly different words or descriptions for the principles. The list of those principles varies from location to location. For example, a school may choose to focus on two or three principles while others may choose many more.

In July 1992, a distinguished group of educators, business and professional persons, and other individuals interested in character education met in Aspen, Colorado. After three days of discussion, those gathered at the meeting agreed on a list of principles that they felt would be acceptable in most communities. These later became known as the "Six Pillars of Character." They are:

- Trustworthiness
- Respect
- Responsibility
- Fairness
- Caring
- Citizenship

On the other hand, Dr. Tom Lickona of the State University of New York at Cortland advocates two words—respect and responsibility.

The state of Georgia has adopted a list of twenty-eight character traits that include:

courage	patriotism	citizenship	honesty
fairness	respect for others	kindness	cooperation
self-respect	self-control	courtesy	compassion
tolerance	diligence	generosity	punctuality
cleanliness	cheerfulness	school pride	patience
creativity	sportsmanship	loyalty	perseverance
virtue	respect for the environment	respect for the creator	

The California Partnership in Character Education has adopted the Six Elements of Character:

Caring	Civic Virtue and Citizenship
Justice and Fairness	Respect
Responsibility	Trustworthiness

Incidentally, the California Partnership's six traits are the same six traits that are cited in Senate bill 311, Feb. 13, 2001. They represent the initiative by President George W. Bush and Congress to fund character education programs.

While these various lists of principles differ in length, they have in common that they contain, for the most part, core consensus values. The importance of creating these lists is to increase the awareness of the principles and to infuse this language into the climate of the school. If you consider the school as an island with a language and culture of its own, then it is easy to see how the dissemination of the principles is a critical element within the overall character development effort.

When consensus on the list of principles is reached, those words must take a prominent place within the environment. They must be posted, referred to, and become part of the language being spoken and modeled.

> Teachers, students, and staff all need to know the core principles for their school community.

Leesville Middle School (Raleigh, North Carolina) teacher Vicki Hedgepeth incorporates this total language model into her writing skills program. She combines several important character-building elements within her program by including writing, cooperative learning, art, community service, and character development. After the students wrote stories based on character themes, they "…painted chairs, benches, and stools reflecting their literary motifs and invited a class of preschool students to experience their creations." As reported by the Character Education Partnership,[3] "Leesville creativity does not end there. In past years, Leesville students have painted a large mural portraying character traits, published a 40-page book of favorite proverbs, created sound montages representing character traits through music, hosted a character education fair, and established a creative project fund to support future activities."

The results are impressive. Not only did Leesville use a total language approach to advertise and promote the principles of good character, they also enjoyed a beneficial side effect. According to the report, "Leesville recently experienced a significant increase in students' writing scores."

In My Experience

B. David Brooks: While working with the staff at Santa Barbara High School in California, we met with a considerable amount of resistance when the principal and I started to discuss character education with the staff. In order to overcome the reluctance, I asked the staff to do just one thing. I told them that we would post two words on the walls in all the classrooms and hallways. Those words were "respect" and "responsibility." The teachers were told that they did not need to do anything except be observant and make note of any reactions the students had regarding the posting of the signs.

I was greeted with rolling eyes and doubtful looks. The principal and I were sure the staff thought that this was an exercise in futility. However, they finally agreed to cooperate.

I returned to the school three weeks later and met with the staff. Anecdote after anecdote painted a picture of positive reactions by students. I was told that at first, students asked why the signs were appearing all over the school, and then they wanted to discuss the principles. Teachers, without being prompted, began to use the words "respect" and "responsibility" in class discussions and in some cases taught writing, language arts, and social studies lessons using the concepts.

Most surprising were the examples of students beginning to use the language of respect and responsibility in conversations. Several teachers related that they had heard students discussing these concepts and in a few cases reminding their peers to be more respectful or responsible. One teacher said, "They were actually using the words."

The systematic presentation of essential principles of good character will almost always affect the climate of the school. When visual and oral displays of caring, respect, honesty, and other principles accompany modeling, reinforcement, and curricular infusion, the climate of the school will reflect good character.

Practice

First, we must find ways to promote or advertise the principles of good character. Second, there must be a conscious effort to encourage the *practice* of good character. As Kevin Ryan, Tom Lickona, Mary Williams, Phil Vincent, and many other proponents of character education point out: good character is about knowing the good and doing the good.

The purpose for presenting the principles of good character is to assist students in their transition from an intellectual understanding of the principle to the practice of the behaviors related to the concept. It does little good to have individuals know intellectually that cheating on a test is against the principal of honesty if they do not practice this principal (and subsequently cheat on the test).

> An effective program provides multiple opportunities for students and staff to put principles into practice.

In structuring a character education program, it is important to purposely build in activities, instructions, and opportunities to practice the character habit and to observe it being practiced by others.

In Chapters 7 and 9 we will share specific strategies for emphasizing, reinforcing, acknowledging, and maintaining the practices of good character that lead to habit formation.

IN MY EXPERIENCE

B. David Brooks: I was working as an assistant principal at Centennial Intermediate School in Los Angeles County. I had taken on the task of counseling a group of students who were particularly mean to their social studies teacher. They could see no reason to be nice to him because he was rude to them.

I asked them to do two things. First, I convinced them to be extra polite to the teacher for two weeks. They were to pay attention, to greet him when they entered the room, and to say goodbye when they left. The second thing I asked them to do was record on a 3x5 card at least three times during class times when they observed the teacher being helpful, courteous, kind, or supportive to *any* student.

I extracted their promise to do this by placing their names in a drawing for prizes of $5.00, $3.00 and $2.00. Each time they brought in a report, I put the students' name in the box. The more they worked at this project, the better their chance of being a winner.

The purpose of this exercise was twofold. First, I wanted the students to practice being polite. I knew that polite behavior generally begets polite responses. Secondly, I reasoned that by looking for kindness or caring actions by the teacher, the students' perceptions of the teacher might change.

The results supported my assumptions. As the students practiced more polite and attentive responses, the teacher began to react to them more positively. I am not sure he knew it, but the students did. The second assumption was also supported when the students started to tell me that the teacher was not such a bad person after all.

I concluded that, at the beginning of this exercise, the students were so focused on what they did not like, they could not see how their interactions with this teacher contributed to the problem. Consequently, when they started to practice polite behavior, their experiences in the class and the classroom climate changed positively.

Process

Reviews of character education programs verify that most effective character education efforts include the presentation of principles and methods for the practicing of the behavior related to the principles. Unfortunately, one of the components of effective character education is generally missing—the third "P," *process*.

The assumption can be made that students can learn the principles of good character. Additionally, they can be offered opportunities to practice behaviors and build habits of good character. Moreover, if practices of good character are reinforced, acknowledged, and supported, the habit formation will take place. However, it is important that they also learn a process for making good decisions so they are able to employ the character skills when embroiled in conflict situations, making a difficult choices between right and wrong, or setting goals.

Almost all parents and educators have asked a child what in the world he or she was thinking when he or she made a poor decision. Often the reply is, "I don't know." While it is a fact that students make hundreds of decisions each day it is also true that many significant choices are made without the benefit of a process for examining alternatives, selecting the action of choice, and basing the decision on an awareness of possible consequences. It is important to know the basic principles of good character and how those principles translate into actions. However, without a system or process for applying the principles and turning them into appropriate actions, the chances of making the right decision is, to some degree, diminished.

> Students and teachers should use a "standardized" process for problem-solving and conflict resolution.

In Chapter 6, we will present the S.T.A.R. process for making ethical decisions, setting goals, resolving conflicts, and answering academic questions.

CASE STUDY

At South Carroll High School in Sykesville, Maryland, the character emphasis is on modeling by adults and assisting students to emulate the modeling in their classrooms and extracurricular activities. David Booz, the principal, believes that students need more than the academics. They must be equipped with the skills of good character if they are to become productive, respectful, responsible, and caring citizens.

In addition to an emphasis on the modeling of good character by adults, the students have participated in the character education effort by incorporating the language of good character into the South Carroll High School's Honor Code. The language of the honor code not only encourages good character, the principles, but suggests ways to practice the habits of good character.

South Carroll High School's Honor Code
Written by SCHS Students

Respect

Respect is something everyone wants, but first, you must give it to receive it.

Actions speak louder than words.

We have the responsibility to uphold respect for people and their belongings.

Integrity

We, as students of South Carroll High School, are expected to live up to the challenge of doing what is right.

You made the choice to be here; make the most of it.

Be mature.

We have the responsibility to intervene and to prevent any confrontations.

Achievement

We have the responsibility to maintain a positive learning environment.

The future belongs to those who believe in the beauty of dreams.

South Carroll High School, a National School of Character, has more than the Honor Code. The school climate encourages all to demonstrate good character in their actions in the classroom. Additionally, many of the extracurricular activities involve community service and charitable work. Achievement, community service, and charitable deeds are examples of translating the principles of good character into practice.

Principal Booz emphasizes the importance of accepting that language leads to attitudes and those attitudes lead to behavior when he says, "If we want them to behave and get along, we have to teach them how to behave and what we expect."

The focus on hard work and character has resulted in positive recognition for the staff and students at South Carroll High School. In 1999, the school received the Maryland Blue Ribbon Award and the Governor's Green School Award for science projects that helped improve the environment.

CHAPTER 6

The S.T.A.R. Decision-Making Process

> **"**It is common sense to take a method and try it: It if fails, admit it frankly and try another. But above all, try something.[1]**"**
>
> Franklin Delano Roosevelt

In Chapter 5, we discussed how language in its broadest sense leads us to perceptions, assumptions, attitudes, and ultimately, behavior. The old saying about the glass being viewed as half empty or half full is based on a true premise. For the most part, we become what we think. If our thoughts are degrading and negative, the chances increase that life will imitate those thoughts. If, on the other hand, attempts are made to look at life in a positive way, then the probability of our achieving positive, favorable consequences increases.

The first two of the Three P's were also discussed in the last chapter. The first P stands for the *principles* that guide a character education program, principles such as trustworthiness, civility, caring, fairness, and others. The second P represents *practice*. In order to develop the habits of good character, the principles must be practiced in the same manner that we practice math skills, social behaviors, and athletic performance.

When you examine character education programs that are in place in the schools, most ongoing efforts have both of the first two of the Three P's. Unfortunately, the third of the Three P's, *process*, is often missing.

Recently, a teacher attending a staff development workshop for the New Orleans Parish Schools remarked that the students she works with all know the principles and sometimes practice them. Regardless of this, her high school students continue to make poor decisions. Although she may not have realized it, she touched on a critical problem. Character education programs are leaving out an essential element for program success if only the first two of the Three P's are implemented: a *process* to help students make better decisions.

In this chapter, we will explore a specific process that can be employed by both students and staff to help them make decisions, solve academic problems, resolve conflicts, plan for the future, and set goals. There are four steps to this process and several procedures within each step. This process is called S.T.A.R., which stands for Stop, Think, Act, Review.

> Students need a specific process to help them with decision-making and problem-solving.

Experienced educators know that, many times, students tend to act without thinking. We have all seen or been involved in situations wherein one student will say something disrespectful to another student, and immediately the second student will react by hitting or pushing. On the other hand, there are those times when a particular student may have learned to stop before acting. In many such instances, an escalation of conflicts can be avoided.

Hasty decisions are often fraught with problems because solutions or consequences were not considered before acting. It is a good bet that at one time or another everyone has said, "I wish I had thought that through before I did it."

The First Step: STOP

STOP, the first step in S.T.A.R., provides individuals with an opportunity to look at potential options, consider different consequences, and ask appropriate questions. It also allows time for collecting or organizing one's thoughts.

B. David Brooks: I first began formulating the S.T.A.R. process while teaching the seventh grade. As a graduate student, I wanted to conduct a mini research project to determine if students who "stopped" before participating in various activities would perform differently than students doing the same activities without stopping first. Since I was teaching several classes, all of which were similar in composition and performance, I decided to present math quizzes in two different ways and then compare the results.

During periods one, three, and five, I gave the following instructions to the class before they took the weekly math quiz:

"Please put your name at the top right-hand corner of your paper and today's date. Class, what is the first step in S.T.A.R.?"

(The class would respond with the word STOP.)

"Class, before we take this quiz, we are going to STOP. Please put your pencils down and organize your thoughts or think about how well you are gong to do on this quiz."

I would wait about ten or fifteen seconds and then instruct the students to begin the quiz.

During periods two, four, and six, I gave these instructions:

"Please put your name at the top right-hand corner of the paper and today's date. You have fifteen minutes to compete this quiz. Begin."

I conducted this experiment for several weeks and compared the quiz scores of the classes. In every case, the classes that were instructed to say the word STOP and that were given a moment to collect their thoughts did better on average than the classes that were not given time to stop.

Mrs. Rosemarie Whitworth, an assistant principal at San Marcos Middle School in Santa Barbara, California, used the STOP step in S.T.A.R. when she encountered students in her office who where upset or angry. The four steps of S.T.A.R. were posted on the wall. When students were out of control, Mrs. Whitworth would point to the first step and tell them that prior to having any discussion or making an attempt to resolve the situation, they were going to have to stop and calm down. It became such a normal part of what happened in her office that all she had to do with many students was simply point at the word stop to get these students to take a few deep breaths and calm themselves.

The Second Step: THINK

The STOP step in S.T.A.R. will give students the opportunity to proceed with the second step of S.T.A.R.—THINK.

"Didn't you think before you did that?" is a common refrain used by adults when they confront children who have done something wrong. Often, the answer is, "No." People who act too quickly and who fail to stop often make mistakes. Once a person has stopped long enough to employ the second step in S.T.A.R.—THINK—the chances are good that he or she will make a better decision.

What is it that we want students to think about while they are stopped? The THINK step of S.T.A.R. is broken down into three parts. These parts are referred to as the ABC's of effective decision-making. They stand for Alternatives, Behavior, and Consequences.

In the THINK step, students are to be taught to use the ABC's and ask themselves a number of questions. There are two sets of questions for the ABC's—one set that is asked before the fact and one set after the fact.

Before the fact:

• What are my alternatives?

• What behavior (action) should I choose?

• What might be the consequences?

After the fact:

• What were my alternatives?

• What behavior (action) did I choose?

• What will be (or are) the consequences?

This THINK step and the ABC questions can be applied to a number of typical school situations. It can be used when students have misbehaved, but it can also be used in academic situations.

Let's look at a hypothetical classroom situation. The class is learning to add, and they have been fully drilled in the S.T.A.R. process. The students can recite the steps to S.T.A.R., and they know and understand the ABC's of decision-making. The teacher has written the following problem on the chalkboard:

$$
\begin{array}{r}
1387 \\
27541 \\
481 \\
+930 \\
\hline
\end{array}
$$

Referring to the second step in S.T.A.R., she asks her students what alternatives they have when trying to solve this problem. One student responds that one alternative is to add the numbers. Upon hearing this, another classmate says that the consequence of choosing that behavior would be a wrong answer. The teacher asks why that would be, and the student replies that a better alternative would be to place the numbers in columns aligned on the decimal place and then add them.

STOP
THINK
A Alternatives
B Behavior
C Consequences

You will notice that both the students and the teacher used the language of ABC from the S.T.A.R. process. In this way, the process becomes part of the problem-solving thinking of the students in both academic and nonacademic settings.

The second step of S.T.A.R. can also be used in conflict-resolution settings. Here's the scenario: Tanya has just pushed Ari to the ground, and they are now both in the Principal's office. The principal has the steps of S.T.A.R. posted on his wall and refers to them when the students arrive. Because both students are upset, he asks them, "What is the first step of S.T.A.R.?" When they reply that it is STOP, he asks them to do just that. After the students have calmed down a bit, he presents them both with a sheet of paper liked the one shown below.

Millard Middle School
S.T.A.R.
CONFLICT RESOLUTION PROCEDURE

STOP	Write a short description of what happened.
THINK	
A	What alternatives do you think you had?
B	Which one did you choose?
C	What do you think the consequences will be?
A	What alternative will you choose next time?
B&C	If you choose that alternative, what do you think the consequences will be

Let's look at Tanya's responses.

Millard Middle School
S.T.A.R.
CONFLICT RESOLUTION PROCEDURE

STOP	Write a short description of what happened.
	Ari took my hat and threw it on the roof, so I hit him and pushed him down. Mrs. Gomez saw me and sent us to the office for fighting.
THINK	
A	What alternatives do you think you had?
	I could have told Mrs. Gomez, and she would have taken care of it. Or I could have come and told you. Or I could have hit Ari and made him get my hat back.

B	Which one did you choose?
	I hit Ari and pushed him down when he wouldn't get my hat.
C	What do you think the consequences will be?
	I am going to be sent home for fighting. And I will get in more trouble at home.
A	What alternative will you choose next time?
	I'll tell Mrs. Gomez what's going on.
B&C	If you choose that alternative, what do you think the consequences will be
	She will help me get my hat back. Ari will be in trouble, but I won't be in trouble.

In this example, the principal has used the first two steps in S.T.A.R. to help resolve the problem. In addition, he helped to plant the idea that there are better ways to solve problems than through violence. Of course, the principal will need to follow though with the consequences and take Ari through the process in order to impress upon him that throwing the hat on the roof was inappropriate.

The Third Step: ACT

The situation in the previous example could easily lead to another type of problem behavior that parents and educators often face with youngsters—"I-am-the-victim" thinking. When a person considers him- or herself to be a victim, then he or she cannot and does not take responsibility for his or her actions. By shifting the blame, the person not only denies responsibility, but also attempts to avoid the consequences of his or her actions.

STOP
THINK
A Alternatives
B Behavior
C Consequences
ACT

For example, take a situation that occurs in classrooms everywhere. The teacher collects the homework, and Megan is without hers. When asked where the homework is, Megan has a number of ready excuses, ranging from the dog ate it to her little brother spilled ice cream on it or her mother forgot to buy an ink cartridge for the computer printer.

While excuses for not handing in homework may seem trivial, the basic "victim thinking" employed while making the excuses is not a matter to be brushed aside. As we said, when people blame someone or something else for their failures, then they shift the responsibility and free themselves from accepting the consequences for their actions.

One way to help students focus on their personal responsibility for their actions is to alter how we discuss their behavior with them. When we look at classrooms, schools, and families, we often hear adults asking youngsters "why" they did this or that. Look at these examples:

Q:*Why* did you push her?

A:Because she looked at me.

Q:*Why* are you late?

A:Because there was a line at the water fountain.

Q:*Why* are you running in the hall?

A:Because Billy was chasing me.

In each of these cases, the student answered with an excuse. The excuses actually removed personal responsibility from the student's thinking and placed it elsewhere.

In step three of S.T.A.R., ACT, we can employ a "languaging" technique that will help students verbalize their actions. Students then begin to understand that their actions are their own responsibility. In the ACT step, adults must shift away from asking *why* and begin to ask *what*.

Let's go back and look at the excuses used by the students on the previous page. In a school where the S.T.A.R. process is taught, understood, and used, the students know that adults will ask them what they are doing or what they just did. Students learn to answer by describing their behavior. Compare the responses.

WHY Questions	WHAT Questions
Q: Why did you push her?	Q: What did you do?
A: Because she looked at me.	A: I pushed her.
Q: Why are you late?	Q: What did you just do?
A: Because there was a line at the water fountain.	A: I came in late for class.
Q: Why are you running in the hall?	Q: What are you doing?
A: Because Billy was chasing me.	A: I am running in the hall.

Of course, this shift in language must be accompanied by instruction. Students must be informed about how the procedure works: When an adult sees you do something, the adult will ask what you just did. Your response will be to describe your behavior or actions.

Kindergarten teachers are great at this technique. A kindergarten teacher will have her students sit on the floor in a semicircle so she can read to them. Then, she will ask them what they are doing, and the children will tell her that they are sitting quietly, waiting for the story.

The shift in language is subtle but important. If, during the ACT step of S.T.A.R., we can encourage students to describe their behavior, then we can assist them in building strengths and diminishing weaknesses. However, this ACT technique gets its greatest power when it is used to encourage students to describe their successes or strengths.

In My Experience

Patricia Freedman: I was walking in the hall at Humble Ninth Grade School in Humble, Texas, when I observed a young lady stop and pick up a piece of paper she had not dropped. After picking up the trash, she threw it into a nearby waste basket.

Knowing that this school was making the transition from why to what, I stopped the girl and asked her, "What did you just do?"

She looked a little surprised and said that she was just going to class and had not done anything. She showed me her pass from the office. I questioned her again by saying, "What did you just do on your way to class?" At that point, she caught on and replied that she had picked up a piece of paper and put it in the trash. I thanked her and told her that that kind of behavior demonstrates good citizenship.

The look on her face was quite telling. She gave me a broad smile and went on her way to class. I am confident that she felt good and will probably continue to do her part to keep the school clean.

The ACT step of S.T.A.R. encourages students to accept responsibility for their actions. If they accept responsibility for their mistakes, they are one step closer to correcting them. On the other hand, if they also accept responsibility for their strengths, they are in a position to build upon them. It is a win-win technique.

There is another way in which the ACT step can help students to take responsibility for their behavior. Look at the word ACT. By placing an "I" before the "A," we can create the acronym I-ACT, which stands for "I Am Choosing To." Students can be taught that they are responsible for the actions they take by having them learn the sentence, "I am choosing to _____."

Let's look at how I-ACT works. When Bill gets to class late because he walked his girlfriend to her class, it is not the girlfriend's fault or that the passing period is too short. It is Bill's fault. Using the I-ACT acronym, Bill would say, "When I walk my girlfriend to her class, *I am choosing to* be late for class."

I   I
A   Am
C   Choosing
T   To _____

Just as we can encourage positive behaviors by asking students what they are doing when they are doing something good, I-ACT can also become an important tool for helping students acknowledge and build upon their strengths. Far too often, students fail to focus on their strengths and thereby fail to build confidence and self-esteem. Some examples of positive statements that build self-confidence would be:

- When I turn in my homework, *I am choosing to* maintain my good grades.

- When I arrive at class on time *I am choosing to* be prepared to start learning.

- When I practice my free throws *I am choosing to* be a better basketball player.

By asking students what they are doing when they are doing right and using I-ACT to have students describe their appropriate behavior, adults will be able to assist young people in building the habits of good character.

The Fourth Step: REVIEW

The final step in S.T.A.R. is REVIEW and is used to ensure that students understand what has transpired in a given situation or academic setting.

As we've discussed in both the THINK and ACT steps, the S.T.A.R. process has two prongs. One is to help students understand and change their misbehavior, and the other is to assist them in strengthening their habits of good character. The REVIEW step can be a powerful tool in helping students see how they can achieve more with positive behavior.

For example, Mike Beck, a social worker in the Humble Independent School District (Texas), used the REVIEW step in S.T.A.R. to develop the Report of Good Character that he uses to reinforce habits of good character.

Students receive the Report of Good Character for demonstrating a positive character trait and are instructed to take the report to an adult for review. In this manner, the students' good character is reinforced by two or more adults.

S.T.A.R.
REVIEW of Good Character

Student name_____

Grade_____

Person awarding this report_____

Reason for report: (Circle all that apply.)

Trustworthiness   Respect   Responsibility   Fairness   Caring   Citizenship

Comments:_____
_____
_____
_____

Reviewed by: (Can be a parent, principal, teacher or other adult)

_____

Comments:_____
_____
_____
_____

Student receives both pages of this form to take to another adult for comments. After getting review comments, student keeps original (white) and submits copy (yellow) to the assistant principal's office to be placed in the student's file.

The REVIEW step of S.T.A.R. also involves teaching students to ask specific questions about their actions. Persons of good character are both personally and socially responsible. That is, they do not justify their behavior with excuses, and they realize that they are responsible for accepting the consequences of their actions. Additionally, they understand that their actions affect others.

In the REVIEW step of S.T.A.R., two questions are taught that are intended to help students understand personal and social responsibility.

The first REVIEW personal responsibility question is: Did my behavior (actions) get me closer to or further from my goals?

STOP
THINK
A Alternatives
B Behavior
C Consequences
ACT
What vs. Why
I am choosing
to _____
REVIEW

I forgot to do my homework. ➜ Did forgetting my homework get me closer to or further from getting a passing grade in this class?

I completed an extra assignment. ➜ Did completing the extra assignment get me closer to or further from getting an A in this class?

The second REVIEW social responsibility question is: How did my behavior (actions) affect others?

I failed my math class. ➜ How are my parents going to handle this?

I received an A in physics. ➜ My mom will be proud of me.

The REVIEW step is a form of metacognition. Students learn to reflect on their choices, the consequences of those decisions, and whether they should have reviewed their alternatives more before acting. The step allows students to plan for better ways of doing things in the future.

Using the Process

There are any number of ways that the S.T.A.R. process and all of its steps can be used to assist students in building the habits of good character. Along with presenting basic principles of good character and helping students practice them, S.T.A.R. will give students a life-long skill for considering options and consequences.

In My Experience

Patricia Freedman: I recently received a message from a teacher, Ms. Mona Thompson, from Atascocita Middle School in Texas. She demonstrates how character education can be infused into the regular curriculum. Thompson is a math teacher and uses the S.T.A.R. process in several different ways. One way is using it to help students assess their own progress.

When she distributes progress reports, she has her students write the steps of S.T.A.R. on a sheet of paper. Then, using the appropriate steps, she has students write two sentences describing how they can use the S.T.A.R. model to improve their grades and class performance. By integrating the S.T.A.R. process with students' academic work, Ms. Thompson reinforces the entire character education effort and helps students integrate what they've learned in math class with the process they've learned through character education.

This is also a valuable tool when setting goals or developing a strategic plan. It is not enough that students know the good and practice the good. They must have the tools to make decisions that will help them employ in a practical sense the principles and skills they are acquiring.

While a teacher at Crosby Independent School District in Texas, Annie Castle used REVIEW in a different manner.

She reported that she had a softball team on a losing streak, and her players were focused on what was going wrong individually and as a team. She asked them to review all the problems they were having and write them on sheets of paper. She took the papers from her players and wadded them up without reading them. She walked her team to second base, pulled up the base pad, deposited all the negative reviews into the metal cup that held the base in place, and burned the pessimistic comments. She then replaced second base and told her players that the negative thoughts were gone. She concluded this exercise by prompting them to begin to review what was going right.

Ms. Castle also encourages her students to keep a "gratitude journal" and review all the things they like about themselves, their school, their families, and their lives. They are not allowed to dwell on the negatives.

It is her belief that we become our language, and if students constantly review what is wrong, depressing, and negative, they will eventually develop habits of thinking that support that view. To counter this, she encourages her girls softball team and the students in her classes to focus on the positive and to build habits of thinking that support good character.

CHAPTER 7

Implementation in the School

"Among the multitude of animals which scamper, fly, burrow, and swim around us, man is the only one who is not locked into his environment. His imagination, his reason, his emotional subtlety, and toughness make it possible for him not to accept the environment but to change it.[1]**"**

Jacob Bronowski

We have examined the foundations upon which character education is based. We have also explored the need for systematic character education and some of the subtleties of moving character education from the invisible curriculum to the visible. We've looked at the duties of the steering committee and the planning required to put an effective character education program in place. In Chapter 4, we touched on climate and culture. In this chapter, we will broaden our discussion with a more in-depth look at various elements of climate and culture. We will also share practical examples and strategies that have proven successful in fostering a teaching/learning environment that is based on a culture of good character. These strategies will be helpful when you actually implement the program you've been planning.

Part of the strategic plan developed by the steering committee includes a schedule for introducing the program in the school(s) or district. Many districts choose to phase in character education over a few years, beginning with individual buildings or grade levels and expanding to other schools. Often, one or two schools pilot the program for a semester or a year before the program is established in other locations. Much of this depends on the district's resources and its ability to administer the program on a broad basis. The case study at the end of this chapter presents one district's implementation timetable.

However you choose to roll out your program, provide sufficient time and resources for staff training—not just teachers, but all staff—from the custodians to the school secretary to the cafeteria supervisors. If the staff is well-trained, then the first step toward a successful program will have been taken. Training can be done by a district's own staff development department or by professional character education trainers. Sometimes a publisher will offer workshops to train teachers on how to best use the publisher's materials.

Make the introduction of character education into an event. Use all of your communication channels—newsletters, parent organizations, local newspapers, etc.—to let people in your community know that you are about to begin this exciting endeavor. When students report in on the first day of school, let them know that this is going to be a very special year. A little enthusiasm goes a long way toward ensuring a successful beginning.

Climate and Environment

According to the *Merriam-Webster's Collegiate Dictionary*,[2] *climate* is "the prevailing influence or environmental conditions characterizing a group." The dictionary defines *environment* as the "aggregate of social and cultural conditions that influence the life of an individual or community." Both these definitions are significant as we look at classrooms and schools. Environment and climate act as powerful forces in shaping the language, attitudes, and behaviors of all members of the school community.

In My Experience

B. David Brooks: Several years ago, I visited an inner-city middle school in Compton, California. My strategy for the visit was to shadow a seventh-grade class for two days. I wanted to travel from class to class and examine how the behavior of the students changed in relation to the culture, climate, and environment in each of the various classrooms. At that time, the school was structured as a five-period day, and almost all of the students remained together the entire day. There were a few exceptions for pullout students and one elective period during which the students went in different directions. Essentially, I traveled with the same students for four of the five periods.

The teacher in period two was a man who stood about 6'3" and could have been a professional football player. His voice boomed when he spoke, and I was sure he could be heard in the gas station across the street. When the seventh-grade students entered the room, they stood around talking and horse playing until the teacher took the roll and ordered them, in a resounding voice, to take their seats. Once they were seated, which took far too much time, he said. "Open your books to page thirty-seven and read the paragraphs. Answer the question that follows each paragraph. Be sure to put your name on the paper." Then he said, "If you need any help, stay in your seat and raise your hand, and I will come over to help you."

Within five seconds after this stern announcement, a boy who had been sitting in the back row stood up, walked to the front of the room, and asked the teacher what he was supposed to do. The teacher, who had just told his students to ". . . stay in your seat and raise your hand, and I will come over to help you," bent toward the boy and explained how he was to proceed. Immediately, other students started getting up and walking about the classroom. Some went up to the teacher while others began to socialize. It took the teacher several minutes to get the students under control. For the remainder of the period, the students continued to act out and very little, if any, teaching or learning took place.

After the passing period, we entered the classroom for period three, a math class. The teacher in this classroom was a woman who, unlike her colleague, was a little less than five feet tall. Many of her students, both boys and girls, were taller than she. As the students entered the room, they filed past a table and picked up their assignment folders. Each manila folder had an activity sheet. I noticed that each student had his or her individualized worksheet. While the teacher took roll, the students proceeded to their seats and began working on their worksheets.

After taking roll, the teacher asked if there were any questions. The same boy who had been the first to walk up to the teacher during period two raised his hand, and the math teacher went to his desk to answer his question. Within a few minutes, other students had their hands up and were helped in order as soon as she had finished working with the previous student. After helping students individually, the teacher conducted a lecture/demonstration for the entire class and assigned homework. The bell rang, and the class was dismissed. It was obvious that both teaching and learning had taken place in this class.

As we think about the two very different situations occurring in the examples outlined above, it is necessary to frame our discussion within the context of environment and climate and the culture that results.

During period two, the environment and climate provided students with an opportunity to move around the classroom, disregard instructions, and generally pass the period without engaging in the learning process. On the other hand, the same students in period three entered the classroom in an orderly manner, retrieved their individual file folders, and got down to work. When they needed help, the teacher assisted them as soon as she had completed her work with other students.

The environment and climate of a school or classroom have a strong affect on student behavior.

The same students acted quite differently during these adjacent periods, and it does not take a rocket scientist to figure out why. Each of these two classrooms had a very different environment and climate. In the environment where the teacher said one thing and did another, where there was an apparent lack of expectations and consequences, the climate that resulted was filled with disruption and was void of teaching and learning. However, where there were expectations and consequences for appropriate behavior, the classroom was conducive to teaching and learning.

Restructuring the Environment

As you think through the implementation of a systematic character education program in a classroom, school, or district, it is beneficial to think from the point of view of the person or persons responsible for structuring the environment. Part of this effort is to structure the surroundings in a way that will create a caring, responsible, and respectful climate. This positive atmosphere will ultimately contribute to a positive culture in the classroom, school, or institution. Taking this view, of course, will mean not only looking at the human environment, such as the interactions between adults and youth, but also carefully examining the physical environment of the school.

IN MY EXPERIENCE

B. David Brooks: Following my presentation at a character education conference in West Virginia, a principal told me about how he and his staff solved a discipline problem by changing the physical environment of their school. They were having trouble with rowdiness in the hallway during passing time.

The school was configured with two parallel halls that could be used for moving from classroom to classroom. For some reason, only one of the halls was used. This meant that most of the student body was traveling in two directions in one hallway during the passing period, resulting in bumping, shoving, and other disruptive behavior. When the staff began to look at this problem from an environmental perspective, they soon realized that they should turn the halls into one-way passages. Students who were going north were instructed to walk in the right-hand hallway. If they were going south, students were to walk in the left-hand hallway.

This simple change in the environment resulted in an end to hallway disruption and greatly reduced the stress hallway monitors were experiencing.

As we look at systematic character education, this example may not appear to fit into our discussion. It is, however, an example of restructuring an environment to create a climate void of temptations to participate in inappropriate behavior. As a school or district moves toward a character education emphasis, it is important to consider all the elements of the environment and climate at the school(s).

An honest evaluation of the school's environment can help staff find ways for improving it.

Think about the term "environment." The environment embodies all the surrounding physical structures and objects. In addition, conditions such as temperature, cleanliness, and ease or difficulty of movement influence the behavior and social interactions of those within that environment. Architects and designers of new office complexes are finding that employees are becoming increasingly isolated because of the computer. Many employees communicate via e-mail or voicemail, and this has resulted in a decline of personal interactions. Consequently, new office structures are being constructed in a manner that requires employees to move through common areas with other people. This design has been shown to increase chance encounters among individuals and, therefore, to increase personal, face-to-face interactions.

As a staff, it is helpful to play the role of a character education environmental evaluation team. This exercise should be designed to consider not only the impact of the interactions of students, community, parents and staff at a school, but also the impact of the physical plant—the buildings and grounds. If a character education program goal is to foster a climate that encourages and supports good character behavior, then the physical environment should support that end.

Patricia Freedman: As the Instructional Coordinator for Wellness for Humble ISD, I spend a great deal of my time visiting schools and classrooms. In my wanderings, I often ask myself how the interpersonal and physical environment supports or detracts from the district's effort to promote character development.

Recently, I had the opportunity to visit three schools. At the elementary school, I observed that the walls in the classrooms, halls, and offices were covered with posters, character quotes, and student work that included many references to good character. The next school, a middle school, had some, but not much, of the physical plant devoted to character traits, student work, or references to the themes promoted by the district. The counselor's office had a few signs on the door and in the window, and some teachers displayed student work or posters that referred to good character. In the high school, however, there was almost a total lack of any physical reference to good character. Actually, the majority of posters and signs were related to upcoming dances and sporting events. Sadly, there was no visual evidence to indicate that good character was important at this school.

Although I was not surprised by these findings, I wanted to take my environmentalist examination one step further. I randomly asked students at all three schools if they knew the character theme of the month. Not surprisingly, only a couple of the high school students and a handful of the middle school students knew that the theme was "trustworthiness." However, at the elementary school, almost everyone I asked either knew the theme or was able to look around and find some idea related to the theme. This, of course, prompted them, and they were able to correctly answer my question.

If it is to succeed, character education needs to be reinforced by the physical environment in all schools and at all grade levels.

In any analysis of the environment, it is critically important to ask questions of both adults and students. For example, is the environment warm or cold? Do the people on campus cultivate a feeling of acceptance, friendliness, respect, caring, and empathy? If the answers to these and similar questions are positive, then the environment for cultivating a strong character education program is in place. If not, there is work to be done to change the environment in ways that will help the character education effort grow.

Advertising, Language, and Character

In Chapter 5, we discussed the advertising model as a way to promote good character. You will recall that the model is based on the formula that language leads to attitudes and expectations, which ultimately lead to behaviors. In this context, language means the words we say, hear, and remember; the songs we sing; the movies we see; the advertisements to which we are exposed; and all the other conscious and subconscious messages we are constantly receiving. Many of these messages, whether we are conscious of them or not, are registered and stored in our memories. In essence, that is the foundation of effective advertising.

Applying advertising principles to the school environment can result in a more successful character education program.

For example, you are walking down the street and a bus drives by with a huge sign advertising a soft drink. The advertising agency that placed that ad on the bus has no expectation that you will stop what you are doing and run to the next convenience store and buy a six pack of the drink. They do expect, however, that your reading of the sign has just become one mental connection building toward a positive attitude about the product. Enough advertising, cleverly done and appealing to your senses, increases the probability that you will buy the product or service. This is a simple but powerful idea. Advertising works!

In implementing a character education program, the advertising model should be one of the important components. Certainly, by putting up a few signs around a school, we cannot expect the students and staff will immediately turn into persons of exemplary character. The purpose for using the advertising model is to:

- raise awareness of students and staff

- reinforce ideals related to good character

- structure the environment around the development and practice of the habits of good character

School as an Island

When implementing your program, consider this metaphor: students travel from island to island each day. One island is the home; other islands are the local mall, playing fields, church, grandma's house, etc. Of course, a big island for students and staff is the school. Within the school, there are other smaller islands—the individual classrooms, the office, the cafeteria, the playground, the gym, etc.

Each of these islands has a language and culture of its own. Systematic character education becomes a bridge that joins or unites each of these islands. As students move from the classroom to the office or the gym, they should be hearing the same language, receiving the same character messages, and having their habits of good character recognized in an identical manner on each island.

> Character education builds bridges that unite the islands within a school.

For some people, the image of *island* could mean that each island is unique and therefore fosters an environment where different words and methods are used to achieve the same results. This concept is a major stumbling block to effective character education. If the people in the office are using one model for resolving conflict and the teachers in PE are using a different model, it does not create a common language within the total school island. An important element of effective character education is the use of common language throughout the school or district, and, hopefully, in the home.

For example, the use of monthly themes such as respect, civility, or responsibility can create a language and culture throughout the school that promotes those traits. However, if the seventh-grade teachers and students are focused on *respect* in January while the eighth graders are working on *responsibility*, the results may be fine for each group, but they do not contribute to a collective atmosphere on the school island.

Common language and procedures throughout the school will result in a culture that supports the development of the habits of good character.

Signage

The use of signage is one of the most powerful strategies for advertising that the school believes in good character and expects and reinforces behaviors indicative of good character. At Atlantis Elementary School in eastern Florida, students, staff, and visitors are met with an array of signs, posters, and character-related student work as they enter the school. Atlantis, which is a National School of Character, prides itself on this advertising campaign. Members of the staff attest to the fact that the signage on the walls in classrooms and throughout the building constantly remind all members of the school community to practice the habits of the good character.

Every wall space and computer screensaver within a building is excellent territory for signage promoting character development. Take a lesson from the streets. Advertising is everywhere. Don't limit yourself; use your imagination. Advertise the principles of character development, common character language, and other character messages you wish to imprint on the minds of students. Use various slogans that are catchy and appealing.

A valuable source of ideas, slogans, posters, and other advertising ideas can found within the school's student population. Students are advertising savvy and can devise powerful ways to get the message across to other students when given the opportunity. For example, at Gulf Middle School in Lee County, Florida, the school was plastered with a slogan reminding everyone about respect, the theme of the month.

Students created an acronym to provide the following reminder:

R	Respect
E	Every
S	Single
P	Person
E	Especially
C	Classmates &
T	Teachers

Target specific populations or areas such as fine arts, athletics, core content areas, the lobby, and the main office. Character development should be an inclusive effort. Don't consider any part of your population as insignificant. Everyone has a stake in promoting good character. Of course, people are busy and cannot always find the time or are not willing to give the time to help with a school-wide character education advertising campaign. Therefore, you must come up with creative ways to implement and sustain an effective school climate effort.

One effective strategy to overcome some of this resistance is to divide the staff into nine equal committees. Each committee will take responsibility for the advertising campaign for one of the nine school months. The entire staff should be included—custodians, teachers, secretaries, aides, administrators, and other staff members. Each committee selects a month and its corresponding theme. By using this technique, everyone becomes involved, and each group only has to take care of a single month and theme. By way of illustration, let's look at a hypothetical example of how this process can work.

The staff at Anytown Elementary School divided themselves into nine character committees at the first staff meeting of the new school year. The October committee consisted of three teachers, a counselor, the custodian, and a teacher's aide. The group was charged with devising and implementing an advertising campaign for *responsibility*, the theme for their month.

The committee, all very busy, decided that two weeks prior to the start of responsibility month, they would send the teachers a memo asking them to have their classes come up with one way that students at Anytown Elementary could demonstrate responsibility during October. Teachers were asked to return their suggestions by the end of September. The committee received the suggestions and placed each of them on a large calendar. For each school day, one or two of the ways to be responsible was listed, along with the name of the teacher who suggested it and the room number. When the large calendar was completed, it was posted in the main hall by the entrance to the school. In addition, each teacher and office received a smaller copy of the calendar on brightly colored paper.

Signage is one of the most powerful tools for communicating positive messages to the school community.

On the first teaching day of October, all school staff received a memo explaining the calendar and suggesting that all adults occasionally ask students how they were going to show responsible behavior that day. The hope was that students would check the responsibility calendar and would know the correct response. If students did not know the way to be responsible that day, the staff was directed to tell them to check the calendar, find the correct skill for the day, and report back. The point was to have the students translate the principle—responsibility—into a practice and then have staff help the students understand this practice by discussing the trait with them. It was equally important that students were able to articulate the specific responsibility skill for the given day.

Although this is a hypothetical example, it is based on the experience of a number of schools that have employed this technique. Anecdotal reports from these schools are very similar. First, the amount of time the committee worked on a project was minimal. In most cases, the entire task took less than four hours. Second, both elementary and middle school staffs reported that at the beginning of the month, for the first three or four days, students did not know the correct response. However, by the start of the second week, students were checking the calendar in the main hall or in their classrooms. Several administrators indicated that the students and some staff saw this as a game. When students were asked how they were to be responsible and did not know, they more often than not found the answer and then tracked down the adult to proudly report the answer. The third and probably the most important aspect of this "game" was the tremendous increase in awareness by students and staff as to the ways a person can demonstrate responsibility.

October 2001

Monday	Tuesday	Wednesday	Thursday	Friday
1 Do my homework. Mr. Carter Rm. 3	**2** Bring my supplies. Miss Thomas Rm. 17	**3** Think before I act. Mrs. Jones PE	**4** Do my own work. Mrs. Pflum Nurse	**5** Pay attention in class. Mr. Harris Rm. 15
8 Play fair. Mr. Williams Rm. 9	**9** Keep trying. Mrs. Clay Rm. 14	**10** Ask when I don't know. Mrs. Bradley Rm. 10	**11** Be on time. Ms. Smith Rm. 5	**12** Put things away. Mrs. Chan Rm. 7
15 Share with others. Ms. Rosenblum Rm. 1	**16** Be prepared for class. Mr. Rodriquez Rm. 8	**17** Stop before I act. Mrs. Gray Principal	**18** Clean up when I'm finished. Mr. Heath Band	**19** Return what I borrow. Ms. Gomez Rm. 12
22 Tell the truth Mrs. Masburn Rm. 6	**23** Study for a test. Mrs. Sage-El Rm. 20	**24** Listen to directions. Mr. Kim Rm. 4	**25** Review my actions. Mrs. Escamilla Main Office	**26** Accept the consequences. Ms. Dinkmeyer Counselor
29 Take my work home. Ms. Korpi Choir	**30** Wait my turn. Mr. Wright Rm. 13	**31** Be helpful. Ms. Kennedy Art		

A sample calendar highlighting the responsibility skills submitted by students

While signage, the backbone of effective advertising, is one of the most important elements of a powerful school climate, it is not the only method for creating a climate that emphasizes good character. There are many other subtle ways to remind students, staff, parents, and the community that character education is an integral part of the district, school, or classroom philosophy.

Student Organizers

The student organizer or calendar has become a staple in many schools. Students use them for making notes, recording assignments, due dates, and social events. In the majority of schools that use these organizers, the schools or districts design some elements for the calendar each year. The cover, rules, and regulations are generally tailored to the particular needs of the school. Some schools have taken this as an opportunity to infuse the monthly character trait into the student organizer.

During this yearly redesign, the opportunity presents itself for including the principles of good character, monthly themes, and other matters that bring the character traits and expectations to the awareness of the student body. In some of the yearly planners, schools have even included character quotes and places for students to set daily, weekly, or monthly goals related to the specific character theme.

Rules and Expectations

The manner in which rules, regulations, and expectations are presented to students varies from school to school and classroom to classroom. Unfortunately, more often than not, the focus on the students' behavior tends toward negative actions rather than those that exemplify good character. For example, most schools have some sort of discipline code that lists unacceptable behaviors and the consequences for those actions. In a subtle way, this disciplinary approach tends to advertise the actions that will necessitate disciplinary responses.

A more productive approach, and one that is congruent with a systematic character program, is to focus on what behaviors are desired, not the undesirable ones. For some educators, this may seem insignificant. It is not. Actually, approaching student discipline from the point of view of appropriate behavior enhances the probability of those behaviors occurring. Additionally, this approach fits nicely with school climate approaches attempting to create a culture of good character.

> Use language that conveys positive expectations.

Returning to the advertising model, think for a moment about the volley of advertising that envelops us and influences our entire visual and auditory world. Ask yourself this question: Do the most prominent advertisers tell you what to buy, or do they tell you what *not* to buy? Successful advertisers encourage the consumer to purchase their product or service. They don't emphasize the opposite.

Take this thinking into the school. Far too often, the rules and expectations in classrooms and schools center on the behavior that is not wanted. If educators want students to behave in a particular way, then students should be instructed to do so. If the goal is to encourage students to act in a positive manner, then those behaviors should be specifically articulated. As is done in the advertising industry, tell students what you expect, and the likelihood that they will go in that direction increases. Character education is one means for accomplishing that goal.

Negative Wording	Positive Wording
Do not run in the halls.	Walk in the halls.
Do not forget your pencil.	Bring your pencil.
Do not leave your tray on the table.	Put your tray in the rack.
Do not be rude.	Be polite.

In My Experience

B. David Brooks: The *Lessons In Character*[3] curriculum for kindergarten has a classroom chart upon which is displayed the days of the week, six character traits, specific expectations for each trait for each day, and the S.T.A.R. steps. This chart is constructed much like a calendar. The chart, displayed below, helps students translate the principles—respect, responsibility, fairness, caring, trustworthiness, and citizenship—into practices. You will note that the chart doesn't display the words *no* and *don't*. The practices listed on the chart clearly state what students are to do.

As you think of ways to promote the habits of good character, keep the advertising model foremost in your mind and state rules, regulations, and expectations in a manner that focuses on the desired behavior, not the undesirable.

Recognition

Most schools have many different ways of recognizing students' accomplishments. Generally, students are recognized or given awards for perfect attendance, academic achievement, and other accomplishments. More often than not, the titles for these forms of recognition fail to attach character language to the award. For example, perfect attendance is a function of being responsible. Therefore, it would enhance the general understanding of the concept of responsibility if the perfect attendance award were to be renamed "The Responsibility Award for Perfect Attendance." Recognition for community service could include *caring* in the title. Student-of-the-Month citations could include character words such as respect, tolerance, trustworthiness, responsibility, excellence, and honor, to mention a few.

Whenever you can infuse the language related to the principles of good character into the culture of the school, it strengthens the character development program. Take the time to align the character language with the particular recognition programs and award certificates. It will pay off in the long run.

Another example of the infusion of the character language into the culture of the school is verbal recognition for a job well done by including the principle associated with the behavior. For example, a student is observed in the cafeteria throwing her garbage away and putting away the serving tray. An adult can acknowledge that action by saying, "Thank you for showing respect and responsibility by cleaning up your area." By using the words "respect" and "responsibility," the connection between the principles and the behavior is made. By the way, both the student and the adult make the connection.

Recognition is important to all people. Connecting the principle with the behavior will go a long way in helping students and staff internalize the concepts being taught through character instruction. The words we use are important and have an effect on the overall climate of the school.

The Character Moment

Due to the nature of the school year, educators often find themselves discarding the innovation efforts from the year before and initiating a new program for the coming year. As we have mentioned before, this mindset often leads to the demise of many promising initiatives. If the character education effort is to continue year to year, it must become part of the environment and culture of the school. Toward that end, it is necessary for the staff to hear how progress is being made and how that process is affecting the overall operation of the school.

The character moment helps celebrate the successes of the program.

One effective method for supporting the character program and infusing it into the culture of the school is to ensure that successes are articulated to the staff. This can be accomplished by including a "character moment" in every staff meeting at the school and board meetings at the administrative level. The character moment should be a standard item on the agenda.

The character moment is intended to be a time when a staff member, student, or parent shares a success story with the attendees at the meeting. This success story is a way to inform the participants about successful experiences related to character education. It is a good-news moment and helps people realize that systematic character education works, is important, and should not be allowed to drift onto the back burner.

In My Experience

B. David Brooks: I once attended a staff meeting at a school where the character moment was a regular part of the meeting. At the meeting in question, a certain teacher asked the principal if she could present a success story. This particular teacher was known as a constant complainer. She was often heard ranting and raving about how irresponsible her students were. Her biggest complaint was that students never returned the pencils she loaned them.

Reluctantly, the principal allowed the teacher to share her story. This is what she said: "As you know, last month was responsibility month. Well, I taught only one lesson all month." The staff looked dismayed as she continued. "The lesson I taught was, 'Responsible people return what they borrow.' Consequently, I have had every pencil I loaned returned so far this month."

The staff applauded.

As we were leaving the meeting, I heard one of the teachers remark. "Wow! This character education stuff really works. If it worked for her, it'll work for anybody!"

The character moment is a time when teachers can share positive events, principals can share insightful quotes or stories, and students can receive recognition. The character moment makes people feel good, buttresses the program, and helps to ensure that the effort will continue.

Announcements

Daily announcements, whether they are presented over the public address system or sent to classrooms on paper or e-mail, serve as one more method to make character education a living part of the language and culture of the school.

Word of the week, quote of the day or week, recognition of students for actions in keeping with a particular character trait, and similar public announcements will instill the concepts of character into the thinking at school.

At Atascocita Middle School in Kingwood, Texas, Mr. Ron Westerfeld, the principal, has followed each daily public address announcement with the following quote: "Make it a great day or not. The choice is yours." He has been making that announcement for over five years. If you were to stand in the hall when he starts the announcement you would hear students and full classes making the announcement along with him. The students from Atascocita Middle School will carry that message with them for the rest of their lives.

On the surface, these simple announcements may seem to be insignificant, but they're not. It is important to remember that the school is
an island, and that island has a culture and language of its own. When
the banners, posters, student work, announcements, awards, and general
discussions reflect the principles of good character, the island will take
on that language and the culture will be favorably altered.

The language of good character leads to attitudes and expectations, and
these will ultimately lead to behaviors and habits of good character.

We have discussed the language and culture of the school at some
length in this and other chapters. There are two other factors that can
greatly enhance the character education effort: parental involvement
and positive adult modeling

Adult Modeling

The modeling of good character is critically important. First of all, we
know that all adults at school are "teachers." Students watch adults.
Yes, they know who is the custodian, secretary, or teacher, but they do
not generally differentiate the adults at school by job classification. If
they see an adult being polite, they see an adult, not a job title. In this
respect, it is important for all staff to be models of good character.

William Bennett, the former United States Secretary of Education,
and Edwin J. Delattre, dean of the School of Education at Boston
University, were recently quoted in *The Advocate*, a newspaper
published in Baton Rouge, Louisiana.[4] Their discussion emphasized the
need to extend character education beyond merely placing a poster on
the wall or having a daily announcement. The article stated: "Teaching
about character ought to occur in the teaching of literature and history,
but lessons about good character are communicated in so many other
ways." The article goes on to quote Bennett and Delattre, "Students
notice whether teachers go about their work conscientiously or lazily,
enthusiastically, or begrudgingly. They see how the adults in the school
address one another, the students, and their parents. They see with

what care (or lack thereof) the school building and grounds are maintained. . . And they learn, too, from the assignments they are given and the evaluations they receive."

Students watch adults, listen to adults, imitate adults, and often remember what adults say. Of course, anyone who has worked in schools knows that students do not always respond in a manner that would indicate in any way that they are listening or watching. The lesson for adults, however, is that we do not know what word or action is being recorded in the memory of the students. A sarcastic, hurtful statement or a supportive, kind remark may be the thought that remains with the youngster for the rest of his or her life. Once we speak the words, they can't be erased or deleted from the student's mind.

A school-wide consciousness of modeling good character is one of the most effective tools for creating a climate that fosters the habits of good character. "Character is taught not only in the classroom, but in cafeterias and hallways, and on the playing fields. The coach who lives by the motto that winning is everything is in character education; the coach who benches starters because of unsportsmanlike conduct is teaching another, better lesson."[5] The probability is that the benched students will be angry initially. As time passes, the modeling of good behavior by the coach will probably become a positive lesson that the players will always carry with them.

As a staff, discuss this vital issue and recognize the importance of adult modeling and the effect it has on the overall character of the school.

Some Final Thoughts

Implementation shouldn't be problematic if you have planned well and then follow your plan. When students walk in the door on the first day of character education implementation, they should sense a difference—a difference in the way the campus looks, a difference in the way the staff reacts to them, and a difference in the common language of the school. Students should feel the excitement in the air.

This chapter has presented a variety of strategies and techniques for implementation. No school or district will use all of them, nor should it. Each school is unique, and the members of the steering committee for the school should choose the strategies they believe will best resonate with their students and staff. Some schools may choose to slowly phase-in different elements and strategies to allow students and staff to adjust to the changes over time. Other schools may want to jump in with both feet and implement a variety of strategies. The degree to which you choose to implement character education and the timeline you follow should be based on a solid understanding of your particular climate and culture.

How you implement character education isn't the most important factor. The most important factor is that you *do* implement character education.

CASE STUDY

In the fall of 1995, the Humble Independent School District in Humble, Texas, began a character education implementation effort that followed a methodology similar to the one outlined in this book. Beginning with a group looking at character education publications and a district-wide steering committee, the Humble ISD has phased-in systematic character education throughout the district. More than a year of planning occurred before the first pilot testing began at some of the district's elementary school campuses. Following the pilots, the district added schools and grade levels each year until the whole district was brought onboard. The entire implementation process took a little over six years to accomplish.

After all schools were included in the character education effort, the district put a new committee in place to look at ways to expand the program in the future. This committee, known as LATTE, which stands for Looking Ahead To Tomorrow's Excellence, is a district-wide steering committee that will make recommendations to the district administration and board. They are working closely with a national character education consultant to ensure that their program will continue.

The table below and on the following page shows the timeline that the district followed when implementing their program.

Activity	Date
Book study group	Fall/Spring 1995
Board info item	May 1995
Initial character education steering committee meeting	August 1995
Second steering committee meeting	October 1995
Third steering committee meeting	November 1995
Fourth steering committee meeting	March 1996
Final steering committee meeting	April 1996
Meeting with administrators at pilot schools	May 1996
Ordered program materials from publisher	May 1996
Planned district-wide staff development	June 1996
Materials delivered to district	August 1996
Teacher in-service training at two elementary schools	August 1996
Pilot program begins	August 1996
Grade 4 and Grade 5 implementation	August 1997
Middle school steering committee begins meetings	November 1997
Middle school implementation	August 1998
Grades K–2 implementation	August 1998

Character education consultant visits elementary campuses	September 1998
Debriefing luncheon with consultant	September 1998
Elementary principals' breakfast	October 1998
Ninth-grade campuses steering committee begins meetings	April 1999
Ninth-grade implementation	August 1999
High school steering committee begins meeting	June 2000
In-service training with all school bus drivers	January 2001
LATTE district-wide steering committee summer workshops with character education consultant	June 2001
High school implementation	August 2001
Board information item/historical perspective	August 2001
The Year of Character proclamation from school board	October 2001
On-going staff development each summer	1996–2001

CHAPTER 8

Connecting School, Parents, and Community

❝From kindergarten to the end of high school, a student's home and classroom are the focal points of their learning experiences. Parents–working with teachers and students–are critical partners in helping a child or children achieve academic successes.[1]❞

National Education Association

Throughout this book, we have commented that parents and the community must partner with the school in order to ensure the successful implementation and maintenance of a systematic character education program. In this chapter, we will discuss the importance of parental and community support. Both parents and community groups can be instrumental in your efforts to help students acquire the habits of good character.

Involving Parents

Getting parents to participate in school meetings and activities has always been a challenge. As students move through the grades, fewer and fewer parents remain involved in parent organizations and school activities. It is a common problem in most districts. Implementing a character education program requires that parents be involved or, at the very least, well-informed.

Of course, one of the jobs is to convince all parents that a school-based character education program is a good idea in the first place. As we have written in previous chapters, it is important to involve all groups from the very beginning. This is true at the district level for steering committees and so forth, but it is also true at the building level, especially when it comes to parents.

You will find that most parents are supportive of your efforts. They will not need any convincing and will be happy to help out in any way they can. However, there will be a number of parents that, for one reason or another, feel a school-based character education program is offensive or, at best, ill-conceived. Knowing in advance that you will meet with some parental opposition can help you be prepared to respond or to be proactive and address many issues before they surface. Hold your first parent meeting early in the school year. Highlight the character education effort by having parents commit to emphasizing skills at home related to the goals of the character education program.

We cannot stress enough how important clear, direct communication with parents is. You must communicate that your character education program isn't meant to supplant what is being taught at home or within a religious community, but rather to reinforce it. Systematic character education does not replace good character training at home; it complements it.

In My Experience

B. David Brooks: At a recent *Lessons In Character* staff development workshop, I had a principal complain about some of the parents at her school. She told me that several of them were upset because she was initiating a character education program. The parents believed that values and character should be taught at home and/or by the church. She asked me how to respond to this concern.

I told her that I have heard the same complaint many times. However, I also said that I have been hearing it less and less frequently over the past ten years. I asked her to consider the following response to the parents. As a matter of fact, I gave her this script to follow:

Parent: Teaching character and values is the responsibility of the home, not the school.

Principal: You're right. The home is the primary place where the skills of good character should be taught and learned. However, there are two things I would like you, as a parent, to consider.

First, as a parent who is taking responsibility for teaching your children respect, responsibility, and other traits of good character, you are doing your best. Nevertheless, if your work at home is not reinforced at school, then your efforts can be undermined. The character education program at school is designed to support your efforts, not supplant them.

Second, you and I both know that all parents are not as willing or able to do what you do. Some children come to school lacking manners, respect, and other character traits that are necessary in a teaching/learning environment. It would be great if all students came prepared to learn, but that is just not the case. When these students act out, are disrespectful, cheat, and create problems, they have an impact on the teacher and on your children. A teacher who is disciplining disruptive students can't be teaching your child at the same time.

At our school, we see character education as a way to reinforce what you are doing at home and to create a teaching/learning environment that makes it possible for teachers to teach and students to learn.

In my experience with many schools across the country, addressing concerns in this manner has almost always helped the reluctant parent to see that systematic character education is a benefit to his or her child.

Inform parents that you are launching or have launched a systematic character education program and, through your newsletter or messages home, offer them two or three simple ways to support the efforts at school.

For example, during responsibility month send a letter like this home with your students.[2]

Dear Family,

This month, our word of the month is Responsibility. We will be working on accountability, excellence, and self-restraint. For example:

Be reliable.

Set a good example for others.

Do your best and keep trying.

Perhaps the best way to reinforce these lessons at home is to give your child chores and expect him or her to be responsible in performing those tasks. The goal is to have youngsters complete their work on their own, without reminders from you, and on time. So when you assign responsibilities to family members, be sure the task is understood and a time frame for getting it done is clear. You might need to check on progress from time to time, especially if the job is a new one.

Also, figure out with your child a regular method for him or her to use in completing homework and other school or extracurricular requirements. Often, youngsters need structure, especially a time frame within which to complete their responsibilities on their own.

Finally, you can set goals for Responsibility. Each member of the family should complete the following sentences and post them where they can serve as a reminder: One responsibility I have is to _____. I promise to fulfill that responsibility by_____.

(Sample goals: One responsibility I have is to do my homework. I promise to fulfill that responsibility by setting aside 15 minutes immediately after dinner Monday through Friday.)

At the end of the month, use the fourth step in S.T.A.R. (Review) to decide whether or not family members accomplished their goals. If you aren't familiar with the S.T.A.R. process, ask your child to explain it to you.

Please share with us any other ideas you have regarding Responsibility.

Thank you for participating.

Sincerely,

Helping Parents to Be Character Educators

There are several messages you can share with parents that will help them raise responsible, caring, civil, and respectful children. You can send these suggestions to parents in newsletters and other communications you have with the home.

Keep the communication door open: Help parents understand that communication with their children is important. However, it is equally important to know *how to communicate* with them. Parents can set an example by respectfully listening to others' opinions. The parent is the ultimate authority, but children and youth do have opinions. When given the opportunity to share their point of view, children learn mutual respect.

Write a note: Children act in responsible ways far more often than they do the opposite. When you notice a child being caring, respectful, helpful, or displaying any one of the many positive character traits they are developing, leave a note letting them know you observed the actions and that you appreciate them. It is a simple yet effective way to reinforce positive behaviors.

Be a model: Parents sometimes forget how closely they are being watched by their children. If the goal is to develop the habits of good character in children, then parents must model those behaviors. Parental modeling is probably the most important example a child has of appropriate or inappropriate behavior.

Review student planners: If students use calendars or planners, encourage parents to review the character themes in the calendar and sign off on them.

Signage at home: Post the school character theme of the month in the home and share with youngsters ways they can put the theme (principle) into practice in the home.

Parent–student projects: Encourage academic activities that involve parents and character education by creating assignments that focus on good character. For example, assign cooperative reading projects wherein parents and students review and explore the character issues in a literature selection.

Parents as Community Resources

Parents are a major component of the community. They live and shop in the attendance area. They work, attend their religious institutions, belong to civic clubs, participate in sports and other activities, and are members of the business and professional community.

The following list describes various ways parents and other family members can involve themselves in supporting the character education effort in their local school. When implementing your program, you may wish to enlist some of your more supportive parents to actively help you in some of these ways.

Make presentations: Parents can present the character education program to local civic clubs. Make sure the parent understands the program completely and has been coached to answer questions in the same manner you would. Involving the parent's child or another student in the presentation can also be very effective.

Work with a church group: Have parents contact their individual religious leaders and encourage their faith community to become involved in the character education effort. The parent can arrange to have an announcement made at services, a short notice placed in the order of service, or an article in the church newsletter. An adult education workshop or presentation could be made, correlating the core values (principles) of the character program to the religious beliefs of the church or denomination.

Distribute signage: Post signs in local business establishments and workplaces highlighting the character traits being taught in the schools.

Work with media outlets: Parents can make an effort to get local media involved in reporting positive character and the work teachers and students are doing to foster the habits of good character.

Read to students: Have parent volunteers read to students from books and stories that emphasize good character.

Support good sportsmanship: Parents coach baseball, soccer, and other sports through community organizations and leagues. Promote good sportsmanship by encouraging positive character and behavior by participants, spectators, and especially parents.

Work on committees: Parents can participate in the school's character education steering committee or other groups that support the character education program. At the building level, establish a parent-run character education committee that can take responsibility for planning and executing the character education bulletin board, character awareness days, and other character-education-related activities or field trips.

Lobby: Through parents, encourage the board of education and the school administration to pursue systematic character education as a top priority.

Character education in cyberspace: Provide materials and resources, such as character education web sites that will assist parents in their character education efforts at home. There are literally hundreds of character education sites on the Internet.

"Embrace, inform, and include" should be your motto with parents when establishing your character education program. Parents are the first and most important character educators. Schools, however, have the opportunity and responsibility to reinforce home-based character training, as well as providing character education when it is not being taught at home.

Involving the Community

There are a number of ways to involve the community in your character education effort. You must keep in mind, however, that the business and professional members of your community are busy people, just like educators. Nevertheless, if approached properly, they are more often than not willing to do their share to help with a character development program.

It is a simple fact that students with good character become workers with good character. When asked about what employers look for in hiring workers, the general answer includes honesty, respect, promptness, reliability, and ability to take constructive criticism, followed by specific skills required for job performance. With this in mind, approach the business community from the point of view that you are teaching character education to prepare students for the workplace. By showing your interest in developing workplace character skills, the business community may respond by providing you with support.

IN MY EXPERIENCE

B. David Brooks: As a principal in Norwalk, California, I designated each school month as a focus month for one community organization or business/professional group. One month might be real estate month, another might be law enforcement month or banking/finance month, etc. I was able to include such diverse groups as lawyers, plumbers, construction workers, union representatives, physicians, and people in the service industry.

During the month, members of the designated group were formally invited to visit the school. Individually or in groups, they were encouraged to call the school and set up a time for a visit.

When they arrived, several students were assigned to the group. The number of students depended on the size of the visiting group. The students accompanied the visitors on a tour of the school.

During these visits, the students were coached to ask the visitors how the character traits we were emphasizing impacted the visitors' professional lives. The students were also instructed to share with the guests what our character education program was and how it was working. We felt that a tour that centered only on "this is the shop," "this is the gym," or "this is the science classroom" would not assist us in helping the members of the community understand that we were preparing students for the world of work through character education.

In my conversations with the visitors following these tours, I was often told that they now had a completely different understanding and appreciation of the program at John Glenn High School. Prior to the visit, they had no idea that character—the skills necessary for success in the work place—was being emphasized.

Raising awareness about our character education efforts led to greater participation in school-related programs by members of the local business and professional community.

Here is a list of ideas and strategies to use in your efforts to include the community in your character education effort.

• Meet with local media representatives. Provide them with a "press pack" that has solid information about your character education program. You could include a press release and perhaps samples of some of the materials. Explain how the program is intended to help students develop habits of good character, and then enlist the representatives' support. Invite the media to your school for a tour and encourage them to feature stories or articles about character education.

• Speak to community service clubs. Members of service clubs are not only representative of the business and professional community, but many are also parents or grandparents.

• Meet with local government officials and encourage them to make proclamations supporting your character education program.

- It is often effective if you take students to meetings with the groups and organizations mentioned above. When students report to adults about how they are learning to be people of character, the audience generally listens.

- Include the entire faith community in your efforts. Along with clergy, involve lay people in your efforts to inform and instruct the community about character education.

- Ask local merchants and professionals, such as doctors, dentists, veterinarians, etc., to post signs at their place of business that support the character education effort at your school. It is helpful to actually provide the signage to be posted.

- Enlist the support of local law enforcement agencies, emergency medical services, and the fire department.

- Bring members of the community into your school to talk with students about the importance of good character in the workplace.

There are many ways that the community at large can assist in supporting your character education program. Don't hesitate to ask for support. The members of your local community can become strong allies. Some of these people are also parents, and many live in or near the attendance area. They witness positive student behavior and share their observations with others. When included, they will do and say things in the community that will increase the probability of assisting your students in their quest to be productive responsible citizens.

CASE STUDY

In the mid 1990s, Mr. Dick Allen, a concerned citizen living on the eastern shore of Maryland, began to look for ways he could help his community assist children and young adults to acquire and practice the habits of good character. After some diligent research and with the help of a few friends, he established a community-based character education project. His goal in forming CC! Character Counts! Midshore was to involve the entire community in the effort. He began by working with the schools and gradually enlisted individuals, as well as business and professional organizations as partners.

The program quickly expanded to five mid-shore Maryland counties—Caroline, Dorchester, Kent, Queen Anne, and Talbot—and included all the schools within their boundaries. While the schools pursued character education programs on their campuses, the effort began to grow in the larger community.

As people became more aware of the effort, several initiatives were undertaken that have resulted in support for character education by the community. Here are a few examples of how the Character Counts! Midshore program has evolved.

- The Easton Bank & Trust includes a character education statement on its bank statements. For example, one statement read, "Can you define responsibility? Do your duty. Be accountable. Exercise self-control. Pursue excellence. Talk with a child about responsibility."

- The monthly bill from the McMahan Oil Co., Inc. recently carried this statement: "Support Character Counts: Respect, Caring, Trustworthiness, Fairness, Citizenship, & Responsibility!"

- The local McDonalds restaurants use a place mat that has been provided to them. The place mats display a number character traits—trustworthiness, respect, responsibility, fairness, caring, and citizenship—across the top of the place mat. A word search and crossword puzzle on the place mat employ character-related words.

- A different place mat, also being used in restaurants throughout the community, encourages the reader to "Stand up for what's right … even if you're standing alone!" and "Set a good example for everyone—be a role model."

- In Easton, Maryland, businessman David Pyles has donated a store window in one of his businesses to the character effort. The window displays, which change throughout the year, emphasize character traits and student work.

- In Easton's Idlewild Park, the bandstand has six columns supporting the roof. Each column displays one of the six character traits of the program in large gold letters. The bandstand is a constant reminder to all that the community supports good character. This was made possible through a unique partnership of Character Counts! Midshore, the municipal government, and the local Rotary club.

Character Counts! Midshore provided spiral-bound booklets called "Take 5 for Character" to community-based youth sports organizations. This pocket-sized booklet presents short character-related situations that can happen during sporting events. Each situation is only four or five sentences long and is designed to encourage coaches to discuss these character issues for five minutes before or during practice.

Here are a couple excerpts from the material found in the "Take 5 for Character" booklets:

Respect & Caring

Your teammate kicks the ball into your own team's goal at the last minute, causing the other team to win. He is upset about it and does not want to talk about it after the game to anyone—including you, his best friend. What would you do?

- Tell him to stop being a crybaby.

- Forget about his being upset, it's his problem.

- Leave him alone for a while, but later on tell him how glad you are that he is on your team.

Citizenship & Respect

At the end of every game, your coach asks that all players thank the officials. However, you are angry with them because they made a call during this game that resulted in a goal that you made being called back. Instead of thanking them, you have decided to tell them what you think of their performance as officials during this game—that they did a bad job.

- Is this the right thing to do?

- What will it accomplish?

Character Counts! Midshore is addressing workplace issues with the booklet "Character in the Workplace," which is being published in partnership with the Chambers of Commerce in the five counties. Similar to "Take 5 for Character," the booklet will be distributed to businesses throughout the area and will provide mini-training sessions in workplace character building.

These are a few of the efforts this community has made in their commitment to advertise, support, and encourage good character. There is probably no scientific way to measure the positive results of this awareness campaign. Yet all indications are that these five counties are coming together to build a community that will enhance the development of habits of good character.

CHAPTER 9

Evaluation

"Every truth has two sides. It is well to look at both before we commit ourselves to either.[1]*"*

Aesop

Evaluating the effectiveness of character education programs has always been a daunting task. In this chapter, we will discuss some methods a school or district might use to monitor its character education efforts. We will also look at research that demonstrates character education does indeed have a positive effect on attitudes and behaviors.

The difficulty of measuring the effect character education has on institutions, groups, or individuals is due to the nature of the variables that must be measured. For example, how can one measure the fact that an individual decides *not* to engage in a fight as a result of learning conflict resolution through character education? The individual is not likely to report to anyone that a fight was avoided. Sadly, good character decisions often go undocumented. On the other hand, poor decisions are fairly easy to count. In schools, we tend to track inappropriate actions such as fights, truancy, and cheating instead of appropriate behaviors.

As a result of this difficulty in evaluating whether character education achieves its goals, available research findings must be divided into three different types:

Anecdotal Reports: This method of assessing character education programs is based on reports from individuals who are in a position to observe student behavior. Admittedly, these reports are subjective and do not fit into the category of "academically strict" research. Often, the results are based on small samples, the instruments used for analysis are sometimes low quality, and the statistical significance is not calculated. Nonetheless, anecdotal reports are important because they are generated by individuals who interact with students and are often affected by student behaviors. Subjective or not, experienced educators know when things are getting better or worse.

Quasi-Scientific Studies: These studies are generally conducted at the local level and lack the sophistication of rigorous scientific research. Although these studies do not meet the criteria for rigid experimental design, they do suggest whether the character education effort is working. These studies can provide a fairly accurate picture of the success or failure of character education programs at a local level.

Later in this chapter, we will review some research that falls into this category—neither anecdotal nor strictly scientific. We report these quasi-scientific studies with the understanding that they do not fit the rigor of academic research nor do they produce findings of statistical significance. However, these studies do suggest that character education results in positive outcomes for both students and staff.

Scientific Studies: Unfortunately, this type of rigorous research is generally lacking in the area of character education evaluations. A frequent concern at character education conferences is that more and better research is needed. Some of the scientifically rigorous information will be reported in this chapter. It should be noted that the lack of this level of research should not suggest that it cannot be proved that character education changes lives and institutions. The dearth of studies merely supports the notion that more scientific research is necessary.

Establishing an Evaluation Procedure

Each school or district needs to determine the type of evaluation it will use and the extent to which it will conduct an evaluation. In some cases, anecdotal reports from staff, students, and parents will satisfy the need for ongoing evaluation. More frequently, quasi-scientific studies, which do not require the time or expense needed for more sophisticated research, will give a clear picture of progress (or lack thereof). The more rigorous scientific studies are generally expensive and require some specialized training. Nevertheless, these scientific studies could be of great benefit to the school or district, as well as the larger educational community.

The first step in the evaluation process is to answer several questions, such as the following:

• What type of evaluation will serve our needs?

• What data will we need to collect to demonstrate whether the character education effort is making an impact?

• From what populations (teachers, administrators, support staff, students, parents) will data be collected?

• How will this data be collected?

• Is there baseline data to compare with the data being collected?

• How will ongoing data be collected?

• How and to whom will the accumulated information be disseminated?

There are a couple of approaches to less rigorous anecdotal reports. These reports rely on subjective input from staff relative to any changes they have observed as a result of a character education program. This review is generally not compared with control populations. However, this type of evaluation can be given several times over a period of time in order to determine if there is a shift in perceptions.

In its simplest form, staff are asked to report their perceptions on a scale of 1 to 5 to a number of questions, similar to the ones following the scale below.

1 None

2 Somewhat

3 Neutral

4 Improved

5 Greatly improved

- Have you observed a positive change in the behavior of your students since the implementation of the character education program?

- Are your students acting more respectfully toward adults?

- Are your students acting more respectfully toward their peers?

- Are your students acting more responsibly?

- Have you observed an increase in the completion of assignments?

- Have you observed an increase in on-time behavior?

Obviously, there are many different questions that could be asked to assess the progress of the character education program. This type of assessment can gain greater credibility if the staff is involved in designing the statements or questions. Each school is unique and will need to look at some character traits that have received specific emphasis in that particular school.

For example, a staff may determine that responsibility and respect are the target character traits that will be emphasized. Therefore, statements or questions focused on those character traits should take precedence in an evaluation or survey.

A second form of anecdotal reporting, the case study type report, involves written observations from the staff. This is a somewhat more time-consuming approach to gathering data and requires more effort in analysis.

An example of this second type of approach is to ask staff to respond to the following:

- Last month was caring month. Please provide a paragraph or two for each item below, which will give our character education steering committee information about the character education effort.

- Please describe how you infused caring into your program or work station last month.

- Please give an example of something you observed which you can attribute to the caring theme.

- Other Comments.

This form of anecdotal evaluation provides all certified and classified staff the opportunity to report the good news and make other comments in an open manner if they feel the program is not working. Research has shown, however, that respondents are more apt to complete a multiple choice questionnaire like the first example than one that requires a more extensive written response.

The Los Angeles Unified School District C has used a survey that fits the quasi-scientific model. This survey is designed to gather pre- and post-implementation data throughout the district. This survey does not directly approach the issue of character education by focusing on specific character traits. Rather, it examines a range of behaviors and conditions that can be considered the elements of school climate affected by systematic character education or lack thereof.

The Annual Stakeholder Satisfaction Survey[2] poses a series of questions at the third- through sixth-grade levels and a different set of questions at the sixth- through twelfth-grade levels.

At the third- through sixth-grade levels, students are asked to respond to fifteen questions with a *yes, no,* or *not sure* response. The following is a sampling of the types of questions on the lower-level survey:

- Do you like your school?

- Is your school kept clean?

- Do you feel the rules are fair?

- Do you feel safe at school?

- Do people work together at your school?

At the more advanced sixth- through twelfth-grade levels, students are asked to respond to twenty-five questions using the following scale: strongly agree, agree, disagree, strongly disagree, and not sure.

The following is a sampling of the types of questions on the upper-level survey:

In my school, I am generally satisfied with the:

- way teachers assign homework

- way teachers grade my work

- behavior of other students

- support I receive from others

- way other students treat me

- way student discipline is handled

While this survey does not directly focus on specific character traits, it does explore whether or not the introduction of a character education program has affected students' perceptions in relation to school climate.

Each district should use the same evaluation techniques and tools over a period of years. When administered pre- and post-implementation and over several years, the results of the evaluation should indicate whether or not the character education program is having an effect.

A more scientific approach to evaluation is to use an assessment instrument employed nationally by a number of schools and districts. One such tool is the Character Education Quality Standards instrument developed and distributed by the Character Education Partnership[3] free of charge.

This comprehensive assessment instrument is designed to be used to evaluate character education programs. The evaluation is based on the CEP's Eleven Principles of Effective Character Education[4] and can be administered to staff and parents.

For example, the statement for item 8.3 is as follows:

Staff models the core values in their interaction with students and each other, and students perceive they do so.

    1 Not evident or visible; poor

    2 Some implementation

    3 Good implementation

    4 Very good implementation

    5 Exemplary implementation

One final aspect of evaluation is the need to assess whether the program is being fully implemented or has lost momentum. A character education program checklist can assist in the effort to ensure that the process is ongoing and maintaining momentum. The checklist can be developed by a school or district and should be based on the elements of character education that are being emphasized by the program that was implemented.

The following statements are samples of the type of items that can help the schools and districts monitor the progress of their programs.

All staff responds to the following statements on a scale of one to five.

    1 Not at all

    2 Rarely

    3 Sometimes

    4 Frequently

    5 Extensively

To what extent is:

• students' character-education-related work being displayed in classrooms and hallways?

- the campus newsletter sharing character education information with parents?

- the parent population aware of character education in the school?

- the language of a decision-making process and the character traits used when granting awards, recognition, and other activities designed to reinforce the habits of good character?

- every teacher involved in the character education implementation in your building?

- a standard school-wide process for decision-making, planning, and conflict resolution utilized?

- character education being taught across content areas?

- character education infused into existing extracurricular activities?

- faculty and staff supporting character education throughout the day?

- students able to define specific character traits?

- the non-certified staff is involved in character education?

The examples above are samples of the types of evaluation tools that a school or district can use. Although many schools and districts do their own assessment, character education program evaluations can be carried out in a number of ways. A school or district might consider one or more of the following:

- evaluation by personnel within the district or school

- contracting with independent consultants

- partnership with a college or university

- state department of education evaluators

- independent research project conducted by an academic who uses funding sources or grants from outside of the district or school

- graduate students to use the opportunity for assessment as a project or thesis

Schools and districts can decide on which type of evaluation is appropriate for their particular needs. The most important issue is that the steering committee commit to some form of ongoing evaluation.

A Review of Some of the Research

As we stated before, there is not an extensive body of academic research focusing on character education programs. However, there are numerous small-scale studies that have been done by individuals within various school districts. Many of these studies fall within the "quasi-scientific" category discussed earlier in this chapter. However, the trends that emerge from these studies are worth noting.

The following abstracts show the kinds of studies that many districts have done as part of their ongoing assessment process to evaluate the overall impact of their character education programs.

The Monk Study:[5] Some of the results of this study were cited in Chapter 4. In his study, Mr. Doug Monk, Kingwood Middle School (Humble, Texas) compared middle school teachers' evaluations of student character before and following the implementation of the *Lessons In Character*[6] curriculum. Results indicated that teachers noted significant gains in several areas. They reported gains in academic work habits, care exhibited toward staff, and increased involvement in volunteer/citizenship projects.

The Thorfinnson Study:[7] This research, performed by Tana R. Thorfinnson, examined teacher perceptions of character education and the perceived effectiveness of a character education program on students' behavior. Pre- and post-surveys were distributed to teachers in three elementary schools. At the test school, a character education strategy was implemented using a *Word of the Week*[8] approach based on six character traits. Two of the schools served as controls. In the control schools, the character education programs were not as well developed. The researcher used the Character Education Survey (see Appendix A).

The instrument consists of forty items related to students' character attributes. The pre- and post-administrations of this instrument were intended to record the perceptions of professional educators by having them make judgements regarding the character of students in general. A Likert response format was used, which employs a one-to-five point scale.

The aggregate mean response of the items was computed for each school. It was found that the mean response (pre to post) in the test school increased $p < .05$ compared to the mean response at a control school. This indicated that the introduction of character education had had a positive effect on the behavior of students at the test school, as perceived by the professional educators who worked with them.

The Lein Study:[9] Mary Lein's study assessed elementary (grades 1-4) teachers' and students' reactions (pre and post) to the *Lessons In Character*[10] curriculum at eleven schools in the Grand Forks Public Schools (North Dakota). The teacher survey asked teachers to describe their impressions of students' character before and after using the program. On eight of the eighteen items, using a five-point Likert scale, teachers rated students' character 20 percent higher after having gone through the curriculum. Responses on four items indicated teachers' belief that students had a better understanding of good character after using the curriculum. Other responses indicated that teachers saw students as having shown more trust and respect to each other. Teachers also noted that students demonstrated greater care and respect for themselves.

The Wulf Study:[11] Dr. Kathleen M. Wulf's study reported the results of the evaluation of the implementation of *Lessons In Character*[12] program in the Los Angeles Unified Schools District (K-5). In the 1995–1996 school year, teams from each of the 430 elementary schools were trained in the curriculum. The data reported in the study (January 1998) was collected using questionnaires from teachers, administrators, and students. Out of the 1,364 teachers who received training in 1995, a total of 323 completed questionnaires in 1998.

Teacher's responses were as follows:

Did you see an increase in achievement among those students exposed to the curriculum?

Strongly disagree/disagree	12%
Unsure/neutral	58%
Agree	25%
Strongly agree	5%

Did you note reduced discipline problems among students who had the curriculum?

Strongly disagree/disagree	6%
Unsure/neutral	45%
Agree	41%
Strongly agree	8%

Did you see an increase in behavior that would indicate that students were applying the lessons learned through the curriculum?

Strongly disagree/disagree	10%
Unsure/neutral	27%
Agree	54%
Strongly agree	9%

Of the 430 elementary schools in Los Angeles Unified School District 245 administrators completed a questionnaire. Their responses follow:

Did you note reduced discipline problems among students who had had the curriculum?

Strongly disagree/disagree	38%
Moderate	32%
Substantial	26%
Great Deal	4%

Did you see an increase in achievement among those students exposed to the curriculum?	
Strongly disagree/disagree	54%
Moderate	34%
Substantial	11%
Great Deal	1%

Did you see an increase in behavior that would indicate that students were applying the lessons learned through the curriculum?	
Strongly disagree/disagree	43%
Moderate	34%
Substantial	21%
Great Deal	2%

In January 1998, pretests were administered to four *Lessons In Character* classrooms for each of the four grades. In June, posttests were administered in the same classrooms. On the questionnaire, students responded to eleven "How Important is it . . . ?" statements. Two items showed consistent growth in percentages of student rating them "very important." On the item regarding the importance of not stealing, all grades showed an increase in the "very important" category with grade four students increasing from 66 percent to 80 percent. With regard to the importance of obeying laws item, all grades also showed gains.

The DeVargas Study:[13] The *Lessons in Character*[14] curriculum was introduced into nine elementary schools and six non-treatment, control schools in the Dallas/Forth Worth, Texas area. There were 182 students in the study sample. Robert C. DeVargas collected data using the Sociomoral Reflective Measure-Short Form.[15] This instrument measures students' stage of cognitive moral development. Although no statistically significant difference was detected between test students and control students on the posttest, it was found that the test students increased in their overall level of moral judgment (pre to post), while the control students demonstrated no such growth.

What the Studies Show

In summary, these findings support the contention that systematic character education has a positive effect in several areas of student achievement and behavior. Positive findings emerged in three areas that were confirmed by more than one study.

Student achievement: In the Monk study, teachers noted an improvement in students' work habits. In the Wulf study, 30 percent of teachers and 46 percent of administrators noted an increase in students' academic achievement that they attributed to the character education curriculum.

Discipline problems: Discipline problems: Monk noted a 50 percent reduction in discipline referrals in his school (data for discipline is shown in Chapter 4). In the Wulf study, 49 percent of the teachers and 62 percent of the administrators observed a reduction in discipline problems as a result of the character education program.

Character development: Character development: Positive findings with regard to students' character development were reported for the character traits of caring, trust, and respect in the Lien study. Monk noted positive development in students' demonstrations of caring and citizenship. In the Wulf study, 63 percent of the teachers and 57 percent of the administrators noted improved student character. DeVargas found that students' stage of moral reasoning increased as a result of the character education curriculum.

In South Carolina, one of the states leading the way in character education, there has been an ongoing effort to implement and assess character education. The State Department of Education has established a Character Education and Community Collaborations effort under the direction of Camille S. Nairn. The Department contracts with Dr. Kathy Paget and Cathy Blume of the Center for Child and Family Studies at the University of South Carolina's College of Social Work to evaluate character education programs.

In July 2001, the South Carolina Partnership in Character Education released the preliminary results of a survey of school administrators. These results are reprinted here with permission.

A survey of school administrators has been conducted twice as part of the evaluation of Partnerships in Character Education, in South Carolina Department of Education's character education initiative. The first survey was conducted in September 1998; the second administration was October 2000. The purposes of the survey were to determine the nature and extent of character education programming in South Carolina and to gather data reflecting school administrators' awareness of character education programming, impressions of the effect of character education programs, and assessments of the trustworthiness of their students. On both administrations, the survey was distributed to approximately 1000 principals, a near universal sample of public school principals in this state.

The following table provides a comparison between the two survey administrations on the characteristics of respondents. Over one third of the surveys were returned on both administrations, and the returned surveys are reasonably representative of schools in the state, with at least 90% of the districts represented among the respondents. On both administrations the respondents represented similar distributions on school type. On the 1998 survey 57% of the responses were from elementary schools, 22% were from middle schools, and 21% were from high schools compared to 59%, 24%, and 18%, respectively on the 2000 survey.

Characteristic	1998 Survey Administration	2000 Survey Administration
Total Survey Distribution	1000	1036
Response Rate	37%	38%
Districts Represented	90%	91%
Counties Represented	100%	98%
Schools with Character Education Efforts	9%	91%

Preliminary analysis of the survey data suggests that character education programming is expanding in South Carolina and that this programming is producing positive results. Most respondents indicated that character education initiatives are being planned or implemented in their schools, and the percentage of schools with character education initiatives was even higher among respondents to the 2000 survey than to the 1998 survey. School administrators were asked if they believed that character education programming had produced positive effects on several variables. Many of them reported improvements in student attitudes (91% in 1998 and 90% in 2000) and behavior (88% in 1998 and 86% in 2000) Eighty-eight percent of the respondents reported improvement in school climate on both survey administrations. Small differences in these reported percentages are not likely to be reflective of significant differences between the two groups of respondents. In addition to these student-related variables, improvements in teacher attitudes also were reported by many of the respondents (67% in 1998 an 62% in 2000). We were not surprised to see these positive outcomes since these are the kinds of variables that character education programs typically address. More importantly, over half of the respondents reported improvements in academic performance (60% in 1998 and 65% in 2000) following the implementation of character education

programs. The increase in the percentage of school administrators reporting improvement in academic performance
associated with character education programs is promising.
Additional analysis of the survey results will include statistical
tests to determine where changes in response patterns are
significant.[16]

Evaluation is a critical element of the overall process for establishing
an effective character education program. Without assessment, there
is a tendency for character education efforts to dwindle and fall by
the wayside.

The first task is to agree that some form of ongoing assessment will
take place. Then, each school or district must decide which form of
evaluation or research they will use. Anecdotal reports, quasi-scientific
studies, or rigorous scientific research are all valuable tools. The form of
research or assessment is secondary to the commitment to conducting an
evaluation that will provide some sort of information. The information
gained from such research can be used to enhance the existing effort,
provide the data necessary for making adjustments, or signal a cause for
celebrating the success of the character education effort.

CASE STUDY

B. David Brooks recalls: While a counselor at
Excelsior High School in Norwalk, California, I
conducted a quasi-scientific study with hardcore truants.
My hypothesis was that personal attention and extrinsic
positive rewards would increase the truants' attendance.

The project included forty tenth- and eleventh-grade male students
who had twenty or more days of truancy during the previous semester.
I held scheduled guidance sessions with each student once a month
and offered them all an open door policy that permitted them to come

to my office at any time. I also gave each student a 3x5 card and instructed him to have his teachers initial the card each day when he attended class. I also encouraged the boys to have the teacher make positive comments on the card. The comment feature was intended to structure positive personal interactions between the student and teacher.

At the end of each school day, the students returned the cards to the office, and I placed ticket in a drawing box for each teacher's initial that a student submitted and another bonus ticket for any positive comments. On Fridays, I held a drawing and awarded prizes such as discounts at local stores, movie passes, records/tapes, and a grand prize of five dollars. This quasi-scientific experiment was conducted over an eight-week period.

The scientific community would argue that this was not good research because I did not have a control group, and I did not keep statistical data. Some would argue that the lack of scientific rigor would discount any results I reported.

Regardless of these objections, I believe that the elements of personal attention and extrinsic rewards for attending class were the factors that influenced a change in student behavior. Of the forty individuals involved, three did not complete the eight weeks and ultimately dropped out of school. Two remained in school but continued to have truancy problems and did not graduate with their class. The remaining thirty-five remained in school. Twenty-seven graduated on time, and eight graduated after summer school or an extra semester.

Regardless of the lack of scientific rigor, I would maintain that the intervention worked.

CHAPTER 10

Strategies for Maintaining Momentum

"The necessity of the times, more than ever, calls for our utmost circumspection, deliberation, fortitude, and perseverance.**"**[1]

Samuel Adams

Putting the above quote in context, Samuel Adams was warning that maintaining the "rights bequeathed to us . . . " will take continued vigilance, work, and perseverance. The same can be said about maintaining a character education program.

For those of us who have spent our professional lives in education, it is sadly obvious that *preserving* and *maintaining* are not always the bywords of program implementation. The pendulum swings, and new initiatives are introduced. Once something has been put in place, it is expected to maintain itself with little or no ongoing effort to ensure the continuation or maintenance of the endeavor. As a result, many important programs die, and the staff returns to old habits.

Successful implementation of character education programs can suffer the same fate if a purposeful effort isn't made to ensure that the program is monitored, adjusted, expanded, and evaluated. With that in mind, we will present a number of ideas and strategies in this chapter that have proven useful in the maintenance of character development efforts.

We believe that a steering committee or staff will find the infusion of new ideas and strategies can help maintain and expand the program, as well as accomplish its goals. These ideas, activities, and strategies are presented here in an abbreviated form and are intended as a "shopping list" that can be used to stimulate discussion. When two or more dedicated educators come together and review lists such as the one presented in this chapter, it is our experience that new and exciting ideas emerge. Some of the strategies in this chapter have been mentioned previously in this book, but we include them here as part of an idea bank for you to draw upon. We are confident that you will be able to use the strategies we are presenting and that you will also generate more of your own.

The ideas, activities, and strategies are separated into four categories:

• School Climate Strategies

• Classroom Strategies

• Parent and Community Involvement Strategies

• Guidance and Extracurricular Strategies

School Climate Strategies

As we have discussed, school climate is an essential part of the overall character education process. Instruction in the classroom can be reinforced by signage, awards, recognition, and activities throughout the school campus. The entire school climate should reflect the ongoing efforts to make character education an important component of the overall educational process.

Administrator Support: Administrators are the primary role models and catalysts for effective character education efforts. When the administration fully supports and is involved in the character development effort, the probability for success is greatly enhanced.

Language: Structure the language in the environment around desirable character traits and behaviors. Make expectations clear to students by using language that broadcasts what behaviors are acceptable. If you want students to walk (not run) in the halls, tell them to walk and then use words to reinforce walking in the halls.

Character Language: Use words associated with the principles you are instilling. If you witness a student picking up trash, express your feelings this way: "That was a great example of being a responsible student." By using the word *responsible* you have accomplished two things—you have reinforced picking up trash, and you have connected the principle with the action.

Advertising: Find opportunities throughout the school to advertise the principles of good character. Students actually do read what is posted. They notice signs and sayings. This advertising helps make one more mental connection to good character. Advertising does make a difference, and it works!

Annual Campus Plans: Include character development in annual campus improvement or strategic plans.

The Character Moment: During every faculty meeting, take the opportunity to share one or two successes related to character education. The reminder can be a simple prompt of the monthly trait, praise for an action observed, or a "good-news" story from a staff member.

Character Calendar: Develop a calendar for the year. Designate a theme-of-the-month for each month in the school year. Another way to use the calendar concept is to create a giant calendar with a character thought for each weekday of the month. Get ideas from students, teachers, and staff. While on school grounds, randomly ask students if they can share the character calendar thought of the day. If they cannot, ask them to go to the calendar and refresh their memory for the day. Make a game of it. Have them find you during the day and relate what they have found.

Center of Attention: Turn your main bulletin board into a character bulletin board where you highlight students of good character, the theme of the month, and some character practices.

Students' Computer-Generated Posters: Have students create posters that highlight the character themes or character traits. Post the students' work throughout the school.

Public Address Announcements: Use daily announcements to remind staff and students of the character trait. Some schools have more extensive announcements with student participation. Have students perform short, character-related "radio plays" or skits during the announcements.

Quote of the Week: Find a quote that focuses on the target character trait. By using the same quote all week, rather than a new quote every day, the students will have a greater understanding of the meaning of the quote by the time they have heard it several times.

The Library: Create a "Character Corner" in the school's library or IMC. Have the librarian or media person concentrate character-related literature and other books in the character corner.

Character Banners: Display character education banners in prominent locations throughout the building.

First Impression: Decorate the windows of the front office area with positive character development signage. The school's main entryway is also a great place to create a good first impression with positive character messages.

Computer Screen Savers: Change computer screen savers to highlight the current character theme. For example, "Bay County Schools—We Respect Each Other" or "Bay County Schools—Our Students Care"

Celebrate with Gusto: Hold a character education pep rally!

Scrolling Marquees: Use your scrolling marquee for character development messages.

Main Marquee: Place the current character theme on the main building marquee (i.e., El Cerrito High School—Theme of the Month Is RESPONSIBILITY).

Slogans: Create a slogan for your school that delivers a good character message, For example, Jefferson High School Royals – A Realm Where Respect Reigns

Respect for the Environment: Connect school cleanliness or beautification with the character trait respect. For example, during the month of respect, focus on upkeep of the cafeteria, hallways, locker rooms, etc. Encourage students and teachers to keep areas clean and neat. Acknowledge such efforts by relating them to the theme.

Nametag Trait ID's: Create name tags with the current character trait or a character trait that the staff member chooses. For example, "Mr. Smith—I value honesty."

New Teacher In-Service: Conduct a yearly, pre-service staff development session on the character education program for teachers new to the school or district.

Character Fair: A character fair is like a science fair. The character fair is intended to highlight activities, projects, essays, community service, and other areas related to promoting good character.

Holidays: Tie monthly traits to holidays. For example, Valentine's Day could emphasize caring for others, or Labor Day might be used to emphasize responsibility.

Student Planners or Agendas: More and more students are using agendas or some form of daily planner to keep track of homework, activities, social events, and all the other engagements that occupy their busy lives. If your school prints planners and can do some customizing, include the principles, practices, and process for developing the habits of good character.

Classroom Strategies

Students spend most of their time in the classroom, so it is logical that the character education effort should have a special focus there. Most systematic character education programs present their formal instruction in the classroom with books, worksheets, lessons, and other activities provided in the program materials. However, within the classroom, instruction alone is not the only influence that impacts the development of the habits of good character. There are many messages, perceptions, expectations, and other factors that affect the total teaching/learning experience. The suggestions that follow will help classroom teachers to identify and implement strategies that will support the character education effort beyond the half-hour formal character lesson.

Teachers Shape Character: Classroom teachers exert special and powerful influences over the academic and character development of their students. Teachers should be continually reminded that their words and actions carry weight, even if it may not seem like it at the moment. Develop a mechanism whereby teachers can recognize and acknowledge how they are influencing the character development of the students.

Homework Paper Headings: Students put their names, date, subject, class period, etc. on assignments. Have students also include a character statement that should appear on all work that is turned in to the teacher. For example:

> Lonnie Carter
> Period 3, Algebra I
> 9/24/01
> I am responsible when I turn my homework in on time.

Make Curricular Connections: Encourage every teacher to make curricular character connections within the general academic offerings.

Character Board: Turn a classroom bulletin board into a character bulletin board where students can be recognized for practicing the habits of good character.

Computer Posters, Slogans, and Web Pages: Have students create posters, slogans, and web pages in computer labs that highlight character themes or character traits.

Classroom Mottoes: Encourage teachers to have students create a character motto for their subject or classroom.

Classroom Posters: Posters either purchased or developed by students should be displayed in the classroom as reminders of the principles, practices, and process for building habits of character.

Lesson Plans: Teachers should be encouraged to include character education as a regular part of their daily lesson plans.

Character Environment: Take time to find pictures of heroes, popular figures, historical events, and people that exhibit traits of good character. Plaster the classroom walls with those pictures and messages.

Writing About Character: Find opportunities in regular writing assignments to have students choose writing topics with a character focus. Stories, letters, anecdotes, and summaries of literature are just some of the possibilities in this area.

Current Events as a Stimulus for Discussions: Newspaper articles and other media stories provide opportunities for talking about both poor and good character. Examples of unsportsmanlike conduct, heroic actions, or acts of kindness are means to foster discussion or writing.

Showcase Character-Related Work: Display all students' work that is character connected. Place it in classrooms, hallways, and main areas of the building. It is part of the effort in advertising character development.

Weekly Focus Suggestions: Use four weeks in every month to build awareness of the principles and practices of good character:

Week 1   Focus on defining the theme.

Week 2   Focus on applying the character trait in school.

Week 3   Focus on committing to the character trait in one's personal life.

Week 4   Focus on applying the character trait in home and community settings.

Warm-up Activities: Brief daily oral or written language exercises can be used to focus on character traits. A short paragraph detailing a character-related dilemma and a discussion as to the solution for the dilemma is another effective tool for focusing on character. These activities are a normal part of the daily routine in many classrooms. The suggestion here is to shift the emphasis of the content toward character education.

Parent and Community Involvement Strategies

As we discussed in Chapter 8, parent support of the character education implementation and maintenance is essential. Parents can reinforce the character lessons when students are at home. By involving parents in the school's efforts, you increase the chance for the overall success of the program. Other members of the community at large can also be involved. People from different walks of life can share with students how good character is important on the job. Here are a few suggestions to get you started.

Inform Your Parents: Notify parents of the character education program that is planned or in progress and enlist their support. At the beginning of the year, send an "introduction to character education" letter to all parents. Explain your character development initiative and invite parents to become active participants.

Newsletter: Include a character development section in your school newsletter. Provide positive illustrations of how your program is working, give uplifting examples, and make suggestions about to how parents might reinforce character education at home.

Parent Organizations: Share your character development program with your parent organization. Have a team of teachers present a typical character education lesson to a PTA or other parent meeting. This activity can go a long way in alleviating any fears parents might have regarding the character emphasis.

Bring the School and Community Together: Create a way to develop a sense of cooperation between the school and surrounding community. For example, encourage community service during the month of caring. Have students perform caring activities outside of the school in order to inform the larger community.

Invited Guests: When guests visit the school or classrooms, inform them of the character trait that is currently being emphasized and ask them to relate that trait to their presentation or talk with students.

Guidance and Extracurricular Strategies

Clubs and organizations, as well as athletics, can influence the overall effort to create a school environment that fosters good character. These extracurricular activities, coupled with the work of guidance staff, can greatly influence the overall school climate by bringing academic instruction, classroom activities, and specific character lessons out of the classroom and into broader areas of student life.

Revise Club Creeds: Campus social clubs should revise their creeds to include good character messages.

Establish a "Character Club": Often, students are looking for outlets to demonstrate good character. Forming a character club (the actual name of which is a local option) will provide an opportunity for students who care about character to participate in activities that foster the character traits emphasized at the school.

Detention: Include character education topics, discussions, worksheets, and instruction as a formal part of detention, Saturday classes, and other programs designed to remediate inappropriate behavior. The students in these "captive" audiences can benefit from positive character messages.

Athletic Awards: Include the language of good character in the athletic awards programs. In addition to MVP, there could be MRP (Most Responsible Player) or MFP (Most Fair Player). Character words are important and send a message that appropriate character traits displayed in athletics are as important the game itself.

Guidance Personnel as Character Readers: More and more guidance personnel and counselors are spending time in classrooms, working directly with groups of students. In the character education arena, these professionals are finding that students welcome discussions about character. One of the most powerful means for initiating character-related discussion is by reading a short story as a stimulus for expanded discussion.

Recognition: Recognizing positive student behavior related to specific character traits is a great way to reinforce and encourage good character. Consider developing awards and recognitions that emphasize character traits. Title those awards and certificates using the character words. For example, rather than a perfect attendance reward, try "The Responsibility Award for Perfect Attendance."

Common Language: Align your building language with character development. Discuss all awards, recognition, discipline, expectations, consequences, goals, plans, etc. in regard to character language and concepts.

Capitalize on Trends: Following the publication of *Random Acts of Kindness*, a national awareness regarding kindness emerged. Capitalize on such occurrences. For example, December, with its various holidays, is a great time to encourage random acts of kindness. One idea is an Acts of Kindness display in the central office or hallway. Those who do good deeds are recognized with their name on an ornament or special card. For example: "Mrs. Bradley says thanks to Mark Schneider for changing her flat tire yesterday." These sentiments can be posted on pre-printed Acts of Kindness Cards and can be done anonymously.

Advocate Character Support: Encourage character development support from all students and outsiders. At athletic events, fine arts performances, and other building activities, display visuals, announce your school's character initiative, and state expectations during the events.

Announcements: Provide an opportunity for students to share their good character experiences or thoughts on character or the trait being emphasized. One example of this is to allow one or more students to end the daily public address announcements with statements of good character they have prepared. Students can be given a prompt such as "Fairness is _____."

There are thousands of ways to enhance a character education effort. We have presented a few ideas, knowing they will act as a stimulus for you to generate many more exciting and meaningful ways to foster the development of the habits of good character. As we mentioned earlier in this chapter, it only takes a gathering of two or more educators to generate an extensive list of powerful ideas and strategies that will support and help maintain this vital effort.

CASE STUDY

B. David Brooks recalls: Earlier in this chapter, we made reference to the need to involve parents in the character education program. There are good reasons for this. For one, when parents are knowledgeable, they are generally supportive. Another reason is to raise the awareness of parents as to the importance of character education in the school and in the home. Busy parents sometimes get wrapped up in grades and other achievements and forget to reinforce, support, and encourage good character. Some parents misunderstand the process and at some level believe that good character is caught not taught.

I experienced, as an outsider, an example of this in June 2001. By the way, this is not an indictment of parents who have worked hard to raise good kids. Rather, for me, it is an example of a missed opportunity to emphasize and recognize good character traits.

At high school graduation time, my local newspaper carries ads with pictures of graduating seniors from area high schools. The ad spaces are provided so that parents can congratulate their sons and daughters upon their completion of high school. Several students are pictured with short notes from parents and loved ones appearing under the photo. All but one of the congratulatory messages carried almost the identical sentiments. The parents and family expressed congratulations, pride, love, and a notation about getting good grades.

However, one particular sentiment jumped off the page at me. Mr. And Mrs. Coram, along with sister Kimi, Mama, and Pa, not only expressed their pride and love but also stressed the character of young Chris Coram when they wrote, "As proud as we are of your academic achievements, we are even more proud (if that is possible) of the fine young man that you have become."

I called Mr. Coram and asked him what that meant. He said, "Good character." As an aside, he, in good character, stressed that his wife had actually written the congratulatory note. Nonetheless he assured me that character was what was important in their family. The grades were great, but the character was paramount.

For me, this is an example of two things. Sadly, the first is the attention grades, sports, and other so-called but fleeting achievements receive. The second is the need for all parents and significant adults to place character above more transient concerns. It may be wonderful that Janice gets straight A's. However, if she fails to develop her skills of kindness, caring, and fairness, the grades pale in significance.

Obviously, Chris Coram achieved in school academically. However, according to his family, his most important achievement was his fine personal character.

Implementing Character Education

CHAPTER ENDNOTES
APPENDICES
INDEX

Endnotes

Chapter 1

[1] United States Department of Education, "Secretary Riles sends guidelines on religion and schools" (press release, U.S. Department of Education, 1995).

[2] Christina Sommers, "Ethical Relativism: Teaching the Virtues," in *The Content of America's Character*, ed. Don E. Eberly (Lanham, MD: Madison Books, 1995), pp. 168–169.

[3] Ibid., p. 170.

[4] B. David Brooks and Frank Goble, *The Case for Character Education* (Northridge, CA: Studio 4 Productions, 1997).

[5] Thomas Lickona, *Educating for Character* (New York: Bantam, 1991).

[6] Ibid., p. 51.

[7] Don E. Eberly, *The Content of America's Character* (Lanham, MD: Madison Books, 1995), p. 25.

[8] Thomas Lickona, Eric Schaps, and Catherine Lewis, "Eleven Principles of Effective Character Education" (pamphlet, Washington, DC: Character Education Partnership).

[9] The Education Commission of the States (Denver, Colorado) is a nonprofit organization assisting legislators and educators set policy to improve student learning at all levels.

[10] Education Commission of the States and Character Education Patnership, "Service-Learning and Character Education: One Plus One Is More Than Two" (issue paper, Denver: Education Commission of the States, April 2001).

[11] The "Six Pillars of Character" is a service mark of the Character Counts! Coalition Project of the Josephson Institute of Ethics.

Chapter 2

[1] Harry S. Dent, *Teaching Jack and Jill Right vs. Wrong in the Homes and Schools* (Augusta, GA: Laity Alive & Serving, Incorporated, 1996), p. 8.

[2] William J. Bennett, "Is Our Culture in Decline?" *Education Week*, April 7, 1993, p. 32.

[3] This survey was administered to the audience at four workshops. The survey contained 35 statements. This is a sample of the responses from the 831 surveys that were returned.

[4] Tony Devine, Ho Joon Seuk, and Andrew Wilson, eds., *Cultivating Heart and Character: Educating for Life's Most Essential Goals* (Chapel Hill, NC: Character Development Publishing, 2001), p. 7.

[5] Lloyd V. Hackley, (address to the National Society for Experiential Education, Gatlinburg, TN, July 27, 2000).

[6] Josephson Institute of Ethics, "The Report Card on the Ethics of American youth: Preliminary Results" (press release, Josephson Intitute of Ethics, October 16, 2000).

Chapter 3

[1] Edward F. DeRoche, and Mary Williams, *Educating Hearts and Minds* (Thousand Oaks, CA: Corwin Press, Inc., 1998), pp. 42–43.

[2] Ibid.

Chapter 4

[1] Michael Hurley (told to the author, B. David Brooks, at a character education training workshop in Grand Forks, ND, September 2001)

[2] Henry A. Huffman, *Developing a Character Education Program: One School's Experience* (Alexandria, VA: ASCD & CEP, 1994), p. 78.

Chapter 5

[1] Hal Urban, *Twenty Things I Want My Kids To Know* (Nashville, TN: Thomas Nelson Publishers, 1992), pp. 2–3.

[2] B. David Brooks, *Lessons In Character* (San Diego, CA: Young Peoples Press, 1998).

[3] Character Education Partnership and Boston University's Center for the Advancement of Ethics and Character, *2000 National Schools of Character and Promising Practices Citations* (Washington, DC: Character Education Partnership, 2000), p. 62.

Chapter 6

[1] Franklin Delano Roosevelt, (speech given at Oglethorpe University, Atlanta, GA, May 22, 1932).

Chapter 7

[1] Jacob Bronowski, *The Ascent of Man* (Boston, MA: Little, Brown, 1974), Ch. 1.

[2] *Mirriam-Webster's Collegiate Dictionary, Tenth Edition* (Springfield, MA: Mirriam Webster, Incorporated, 1993).

[3] B. David Brooks, *Lessons In Character* (San Diego, CA: Young Peoples Press, Inc., 1996).

[4] "Teaching Character," *The Advocate OnLine* (www.theadvocate.com), August 31, 2001.

[5] Ibid.

Chapter 8

[1] "Items to Duplicate, Distribute, and Post," National Education Association (www.nea.org/aew/items.html).

[2] Taken from "Family Letters," *Lessons in Character Administrators Package* (San Diego, CA: Young People's Press, Inc., 1998).

Chapter 9

[1] from Aesop's fables as quoted in "Daily Announcements," *Lessons in Character Administrators Package* (San Diego, CA: Young People's Press, Inc., 1998).

[2] Los Angeles Unified School District, District, "The Annual Stakeholder Satisfaction Survey (Grades 3–6 and 6–12)" (LAUSD, C. Robert J. Collins, Superintendent, revised 1/1996).

[3] The Character Education Quality Standards evaluation instrument is published and distributed at no charge by CEP.
Copies of the instrument can be obtained by contacting the organization: Character Education Partnership, 1600 K Street NW, Suite 501, Washington, DC 20006.
Phone: (800) 988-8081. FAX (202) 296-7779.
The document can also be downloaded from the CEP website: www.character.org.

[4] Thomas Lickona, Eric Schaps, and Catherine Lewis, "Eleven Principles of Effective Character Education" (pamphlet, Washington, DC: Character Education Partnership).

[5] Douglas Monk, "Pre-post Survey of Middle School Teachers" (Humble, TX: Humble Independent School District, 1999).

[6] B. David Brooks, *Lessons In Character* (San Diego, CA: Young People's Press, Inc., 1998).

[7] Tana R. Thorfinnson, "Teacher's Perceptions of a Character Education Program" (master's thesis, University of North Dakota, Grand Forks, 2000).

[8] Ken Newbury, *Word of the Week* (San Diego, CA: Young People's Press, Inc., 1998).

[9] Mary Lein, "Character Education Survey Report" (Grand Forks, ND: Grand Forks Public Schools, 2000).

[10] Brooks, op. cit.

[11] Kathleen M. Wulf, "An Evaluation of the *Lessons in Character* Character Education Program: Final Report" (Pacific Palisades: CA: Wulf Educational Services, 1998).

[12] Brooks, op. cit.

[13] Robert C. DeVargas, "A Study of *Lessons in Character*: The Effect of Moral Development Curriculum upon Moral Judgment" (Fort Worth, TX: Southwest Baptist Theological Seminary, 1998).

[14] Brooks, op. cit.

[15] John C. Gibbs, Karen S. Basinger, and Dick Fuller, *Moral Maturity: Measuring the Development of Sociomoral Reflections* (Hillsdale, NJ: Lawrence Erlbaum Associates, 1992).

[16] Cathy Blume and Kathy Paget, "Partnerships in Character Education Survey of School Administrators Preliminary Results" (Center for Child and Family Services at the University of South Carolina, photocopy, 2001).

Chapter 10

[1] Samuel Adams [writing under the pseudonym Candidus] *Boston Gazette*, October 14, 1771. Some sources attribute this quote to a speech Adams made in Boston, however it is believed that he wrote the essay for the *Boston Gazette* first and then used the essay as a source for his speech.

Character Education Survey

Date Administered_____   Pre_____   Post_____

Character Education Defined: Character education is the systematic teaching of basic character traits and skills such as trustworthiness, punctuality, respect for self and others, caring, perseverance, citizenship, and other common core attributes.

Character education, as used in this survey, relates to the systematic teaching of common core character traits and skills as a stand-alone, identifiable curriculum and/or a viable curriculum infused into core subject matter lessons.

Please respond to the following statements from the viewpoint of education *in general* or schools *in general* and *not* from the perspective of your school, your school district, or your children/family.

Indicate your agreement or disagreement with the following statements on a scale of 1 to 5, with 1 indicating strong agreement and 5 indicating strong disagreement.

	Strongly Agree 1	2	3	4	Strongly Disagree 5
1. Students are trustworthy.					
2. Cheating is rare at this school.					
3. Students trust each other.					
4. Teachers can trust students to be responsible.					
5. Students can describe the characteristics of a trustworthy person.					
6. Overall, students are responsible.					
7. Students can be counted on to do as expected.					
8. Students complete their assignments on their own.					
9. Students are responsible even when they are not being monitored.					
10. Students can describe a responsible person.					
11. Students display caring behavior toward each other.					
12. Students display caring behavior toward staff.					
13. Students take care when completing assignments.					
14. Students appear to care for themselves, which shows up in appearance and what they say about themselves.					
15. Students can describe a caring person.					
16. Students are respectful toward each other.					
17. Students are respectful toward staff.					
18. Students display respect for themselves as seen through their appearance and how they talk about themselves.					

	Strongly Agree				Strongly Disagree
	1	2	3	4	5
19. Students react respectfully when disciplined.					
20. Students can describe a respectful person.					
21. Students display fairness in their interactions with each other.					
22. Students are fair in evaluating their own actions.					
23. Students view discipline codes, rules, and procedures as fair.					
24. Students participate fairly during athletic activities and treat opponents fairly.					
25. Students can describe a fair person.					
26. Students are aware of the citizenship requirements for success at school.					
27. Students participate in school activities such as clubs, student government, and related citizenship activities.					
28. Students initiate and participate in good-citizenship projects.					
29. Students participate in volunteer activities in and out of school.					
30. Students can describe a person who is a good citizen.					
31. Students have a mental process for making decisions.					
32. Students are aware of the steps to be taken in resolving conflicts.					
33. Students actually use a systematic decision-making, conflict-resolution, or anger-management process.					
34. When asked about inappropriate behavior, students can articulate the path they took to arrive at the particular behavior.					
35. When asked about inappropriate behavior, students can articulate what they perceive as possible consequences for the behavior					
36. Students are less respectful than they were 15 years ago.					
37. Students tend to use violence as a means for solving problems or resolving conflicts more often than they did 15 years ago.					
38. Manners have declined over the past 15 years.					
39. Schools are not longer the safe havens they once were for students.					
40. Problems of disrespect and irresponsibility are just as serious in rural areas as they are in urban areas.					

Student Character Education Survey

Administration instructions for this survey:

The survey contains twelve basic statements. Following each statement is an example of a typical response elicited from students.

Instruct the students to carefully read each statement and fill in the blank spaces below the statement. Listed below are typical responses to each statement. This is not an exhaustive list. Student responses will vary. In scoring this survey, you will need to use your judgement as to whether or not a response is accurate.

The purpose of the survey is to assess whether or not students have a general understanding of what behaviors relate to each of the character traits.

A person who is not trustworthy will: Betray a trust, deceive, mislead, cheat, steal, do things that are wrong, talk behind people's backs, do anything to win a friendship.

A person who is trustworthy will: Keep his/her word, tell the truth, be sincere, stand up for his/her beliefs, show commitment, have courage, stand by a friend, honor commitments.

A person who is not respectful will: Mistreat people, abuse, demean, manipulate, exploit, take advantage of others, be judgmental and prejudiced.

A person who is respectful will: Accept others, judge people on their merits, be courteous and polite, appreciate and accept individual differences, respect the rights of others.

A person who is not responsible will: Make excuses, blame others for his/her mistakes, take credit for others' achievements, quit or give up easily.

A person who is responsible will: Do his/her best, think before they act, consider the consequences of his/her actions, think of how his/her behavior affects others, be reliable, be accountable, accept responsibility, set a good example, keep commitments.

A person who is not fair will: Laugh at the mistakes of others, take advantage of others, cheat at games, take more than his/her share, be closed-minded, make decisions without considering others.

A person who is fair will: Listen to others, treat others as he/she would want to be treated, be open-minded, consider others, try to understand how the other person feels, make decisions after considering others, understand when people make mistakes.

A person who is not caring will: Be mean to others, be selfish, overlook the feelings of others, be cruel to others, tease and make fun of others, do whatever he/she wants without thinking of how it affects others.

A person who is caring will: Help others, show he/she cares for others by being kind, share with others, show that he/she understands how other people are feeling when they are sad or hurt, be helpful.

A person who is not a good citizen will: Disobey rules, cheat on tests, make false statements, fail to cooperate with the group, mislead people by not telling the whole truth, litter.

A person who is a good citizen will: Play by the rules, obey just laws, do his/her share, respect authority, stay informed, vote, be charitable, protect the environment, conserve natural resources.

This survey should be administered **prior to the introduction of a character education curriculum** and again at the **end of one school year of the program**. The survey is designed to determine whether or not students acquire knowledge of behaviors related to the character traits of trustworthiness, respect, responsibility, fairness, caring, and citizenship.

Combining the results of this pre-post survey with objective criteria, such as the decline or increase in referrals for major or minor discipline problems, attendance, tardiness, number of students on the honor roll, and other objective criteria will provide you with information that will assist you in evaluating the effectiveness of your systematic character education efforts.

Student Character Education Survey

Below you will find a number of statements. Read each statement carefully and complete the statement by filling in the blank spaces.

A person who *is not* trustworthy will:
1. break a promise.
2. _____
3. _____
4. _____
5. _____

A person who *is* trustworthy will:
1. keep his or her word.
2. _____
3. _____
4. _____
5. _____

A person who *is not* respectful will:
1. mistreat people.
2. _____
3. _____
4. _____
5. _____

A person who *is* respectful will:
1. accept others.
2. _____
3. _____
4. _____
5. _____

A person who *is not* responsible will:
1. make excuses.
2. _____
3. _____
4. _____
5. _____

A person who *is* responsible will:
1. do his or her best.
2. _____
3. _____
4. _____
5. _____

A person who *is not* fair will:
1. laugh at the mistakes of others.
2. _____
3. _____
4. _____
5. _____

A person who *is* fair will:
1. listen to others.
2. _____
3. _____
4. _____
5. _____

A person who *is not* caring will:
1. be mean to others.
2. _____
3. _____
4. _____
5. _____

A person who *is* caring will:
1. help others.
2. _____
3. _____
4. _____
5. _____

A person who *is not* a good citizen will:
1. disobey rules.
2. _____
3. _____
4. _____
5. _____

A person who *is* a good citizen will:
1. play by the rules.
2. _____
3. _____
4. _____
5. _____

Organizations Involved with Character Education

American Association of School Administrators
1801 North Moore Street
Alexandria, VA 22209-9988
(703) 528-0700
www.aasa.org

American Federation of Teachers
555 New Jersey Avenue, NW
Washington, DC 20001
(202) 393-6374
www.aft.org

American Youth Foundation
315 Ann Avenue
St. Louis, MO 63104
(314) 772-8626
www.afy.com

Association for Moral Education
205 Development Center
PO Box 870158
University of Alabama
Birmingham, AL 35487
(205) 348-8146
www4.wittenberg.edu/ame

Association for Supervision and Curriculum Development
1250 North Pitt Street
Alexandria, VA 22314
(703) 549-9110
www.ascd.org

The Ruby Bridges Educational Foundation
PO Box 870248
New Orleans, Louisiana 70187

Career Solutions Training Group
3 East Central Avenue
Paoli, PA 19301
(610) 993-8292
www.careersolutionsgroup.com

Center for Civic Education
5146 Douglas Fir Road
Calabasas, CA 91302-1467
(800) 350-4223
www.civiced.org

Center for Ethical Leadership
464 12th Avenue, Suite 320
Seattle, WA 98122
(206)328-3020
www.ethicalleadership.org

Center for Ethics and Workplace Readiness
2433 Thomas Drive, PMB106
Panama City Beach, FL 32408
(877) 214-7974
www.bdavidbrooks.com

Center for Learning
21590 Center Ridge Road
Rocky River, OH 44116
(216) 331-1404
www.centerforlearning.org

Center for the Advancement of Ethics and Character
School of Education
Boston University 605
Commonwealth Avenue
Boston, MA 02215
(617) 353-3262
www.bu.edu/www/c4n5rs

Center for the 4th and 5th Rs
P.O. Box 2000
SUNY Cortland
Education Department
Cortland, NY 13045
(607) 753-2456
www.cortland.edu/www/c4n5rs/home.htm

Character Development Foundation
PO Box 4782
Manchester, NH 03108-4782
(603) 472-3063
www.charactered.org

Character Education Institute
8918 Tesoro Drive, Suite 575
San Antonio, TX 78217-6253
(800) 284-0499
www.charactereducation.org

Character Education Institute at California University
250 University Avenue
California, PA 15419-1394
(412) 938-4500
www.cup.edu/education/charactered

Character Education Partnership
918 16th Street, NW, Suite 501
Washington, DC 20006
(800) 988-8081
http://www.character.org

Character Development Group
PO Box 9211
Chapel Hill, NC 27515-9211
(919) 967-2110
www.charactereducation.com

Chicago Foundation for Education
400 N. Michigan Avenue, Room 311
Chicago, IL 60611
(312) 670-2323
www.chgofdnedu.org

Close-Up Foundation
44 Canal Center Plaza
Alexandria, VA 22314
(703) 706-3330
www.closeup.org

The Communitarian Network
2130 H Street, NW #714-X
Washington, DC 20052
(202) 994-8142
www.gwu.edu/~ccps

Community of Caring
Joseph P. Kennedy Jr. Foundation
1325 G Street, NW #500
Washington, DC 20005
(202) 393-1250
www.familyvillage.wisc.edu/jpkf

Developing Resources for Education in America, Inc. (DREAM)
817 E. River Place
Jackson, MS 39202
(800) 233-7326
www.dreaminc.org

Developmental Studies Center
2000 Embarcadero, Suite 305
Oakland, CA 94606
(510) 533-0213
www.devstu.org

Dream Builders
PO Box 70906
Marrietta, GA 30007
(800) 524-2813

Educators for Social Responsibility
23 Garden Street
Cambridge, MA 02138
(617) 492-1764
www.esrnational.org

Ethics Resource Center
1747 Pennsylvania Avenue, Suite 400
Washington, DC 20006
(202) 737-2258
www.ethics.org

The Giraffe Project
P.O. Box 759
Langley, WA 98260
(360) 221-7989
www.giraffe.org/giraffe/

Heartwood Institute
425 N. Craig Street, Suite 302
Pittsburgh, PA 15213
(800) 432-7810
www.heartwoodethics.org/

Home and School Institute
MegaSkills Education Center
1500 Massachusetts Avenue, NW
Washington, DC 20005
(202) 466-3633
www.megaskillsi.org

IllumniQuest
10314 Mystic Meadow Way
Oakton, VA 22124
(703) 255-7200

The Institute for Global Ethics
11/13 Main Street
Camden, ME 04843
(207) 236-6658
www.globalethics.org

International Education Foundation
4 West 43rd Street
New York, NY 10036
(212) 944-7466

Josephson Institute of Ethics
4640 Admiralty Way #1000
Marina del Rey, CA 90292-6610
(310) 306-1868
www.josephsoninstitute.org

Learning for Life
Boy Scouts of America
1325 W. Walnut Hill Lane
Irving, TX 75015-2079
(972) 580-2428
www.bsa.org

Legacy Learning
1810 Hardison Place #10
South Pasadena, CA 91030
(818) 441-7944

National Association of Elementary School Principals
1615 Duke Street
Alexandria, VA 22314
(800) 386-2377
www.aesp.org

National Association of Partners in Education
901 North Pitt Street
Suite 320, Alexandria, VA 22314
(703) 836-4880
www.napehq.org

National Association of Secondary School Principals
1904 Association Drive
Reston, VA 22091
(800) 253-7746
www.nassp.org

National Education Association
1201 Sixteenth Street, NW
Suite 800
Washington, DC 20036
(202) 833-4000
www.nea.org

National School Boards Association
1680 Duke Street
Alexandria, VA 22314
(703) 838-6722
www.nsba.org

National Youth Leadership Council
1910 West County Road B
Roseville, MN 55113
(612) 631-3672
www.nylc.org

National Council for the Social Studies
3501 Newark Street, NW
Washington, DC 20016-3167
(202) 966-7840
www.ncss.org

No Putdowns-CONTACT
3049 East Genesee Street
Syracuse, NY 13244
(800) 561-4571
www.noputdowns.org

Northeast Foundation for Children
71 Montague City Road
Greenfield, MA 01301
(800) 360-6332
www.responsiveclassroom.org

Northwest Center for Philosophy for Children
Box 353350
Department of Philosophy
University of Washington
Seattle, WA 98195-3350
(206) 463-1217

Phi Delta Kappa
PO Box 789
Bloomington, IN 47402
(800) 766-1156

Positive Action Company
264 Fourth Avenue South
Twin Falls, ID 83301
(800) 345-2974

Personal Responsibility Education Process (PREP)
Cooperating School Districts of Greater St. Louis
13157 Olive Spur Road
St. Louis, MO 63141
(314) 576-3535 ext. 310

Project Service Leadership
12703 NW 20th Avenue
Vancouver, WA 98685
(360) 750-7500

Quest International
32 South Street, Suite 500
Baltimore, MD 21202
(800) 446-2700
www.quest.edu

School for Ethical Education
440 Wheelers Farm Road
Milford, CT 06460
(203) 783-4439
www.ethicsed.org

Southern Poverty Law Center
400 Washington Avenue
Montgomery, AL 36104
(334) 956-8200
www.splcenter.org

Students Taking a Right Stand (STARS)
Center for Youth Issues, Inc.
P.O. Box 22185
ChattanoogaTN 37422-2185
(800) 477-8277
www.cyi-stars.org

Teel Institute
101 East Armour Blvd.
Kansas City, MO 64111
(816) 753-2733

Virtues Project
727 Johnson Street, Suite G
Victoria, BC V8W 1MG
(250) 382-8300
www.virtuesproject.com

Washington State Partnership on Character Education
OSPI
PO Box 47200
Olympia, WA 98504-7200
(360) 664-2534
www.etdc.wednet.edu/character

Young People's Press
3033 Fifth Avenue, Suite 200
San Diego, CA 92103
(800) 231-9774
www.youngpeoplespress.com

Your Environment Inc.
704 Monongahela Avenue
Glassport, PA 15045-1625
(412) 466-2240

Youth Frontiers, Inc.
6009 Excelsior Blvd.
Minneapolis, MN 55416
(952) 922-0222
www.youthfrontiers.org

Funding Sources

Funding for character education can come from a variety of sources. For a number of years, the United States Office of Education has funded specific character education projects. There have also been grants that have come from the department's discretionary funds. School systems should not, however, rely on federal grants alone. During the past few years, almost all states have provided some level of funding for character education. In addition, business, industry, civic, and service organizations have supported character education efforts that have fit within their philosophies.

Character education has now been included as a category under Safe and Drug Free Schools grants from federal monies, school-to-work initiatives, and other safe school programs. In addition, many states are allocating staff development funding for use in the area of character or values education.

Grant requirements and funding opportunities vary from state to state, agency to agency, and year to year. The most effective way to seek out grants or funding sources is to contact your state department of education, search via the Internet, or check with some of the sources we have provided.

Listed below are a number of resources for you to use in researching funding opportunities for character education. Although the list is not exhaustive, it will open other links to funding sources.

Business and Professional Community

Character education is directly tied to the skills necessary for success in the workplace. When seeking funding for local character education projects, do not fail to look to your local business and professional community. This includes many different service organizations such as Rotary, Kiwanis, Lions, etc. An emphasis on character skills as they relate to future employees is a strategy that has often resulted in local funding of character education curriculum and/or training.

United States Department of Education

Federal dollars for character education have in the past (and will likely continue into the future) come from the following United States Department Of Education sources: Title I, Title II, Title IV, Title VI, special education, drop-out prevention programs, and professional development grants. The office of Safe and Drug Free Schools has provided character education grants nationally.

U.S. Dept. of Education
400 Maryland Ave, SW
Washington, DC 20202
1-800-872-5327
http://www.ed.gov/GrantApps
http://www.ed.gov/funding.html

Internet Resources

Google
http://www.google.com
> Google is an excellent search engine that can provides a comprehensive list of character education state funding web pages and many other character education funding sources. Search under "character education funding" or "character education funds."

School Grants
http://www.schoolgrants.org
> This is a one-stop site for schools. It provides links to state and federal agencies, foundations, and grant writing resources.

Society of Research Administrator's Grants Website
http://sra.rams.com/cus/sra/resource.htm
> This is an excellent source for government and private grants. You can search for grant focus (k-12) and private funding.

Foundation Center
http://www.fdncenter.org
> This site offers a directory of over 1,000 websites concerning grants for educational initiatives. It includes information and links to private and community foundations, corporate grants, and public charities.

Corporation of Public Broadcasting
http://www.cpb.org/grants/grantwriting.html
> This site is easy to use and guides the user through the elements of grant writing. It offers guideposts to assist you through the grant writing process.

Foundations on Line
http://www.foundations.org
> Foundations on Line offers a comprehensive list of corporate- and community-based foundations that have funding available. This site is not searchable by topic. Many of the grants are general in nature and the grant writer can adapt his or her application the meet the criteria of the granting organization.

Selected Bibilography

Akin, Terri. *Character Education in America's Schools*. Spring Valley, CA: Innerchoice Publications, 1995.

Albert, Linda A. *Cooperative Discipline*. Circle Pines, MN: American Guidance Service, 1996.

Bennett, William. *The Book of Virtues: A Treasury of Great Moral Stories*. New York: Simon and Schuster, 1995.

Bennett, William. *The Moral Compass*. New York: Simon and Schuster, 1995.

Brooks, B. David and Frank Goble. *The Case for Character Education*. Northridge, CA: Studio 4 Productions, 1997.

Charney, Ruth Sidney. *Teaching Children to Care: Management in the Responsive Classroom*. Greenfield, MA: Northeast Foundation for Children 1992.

Coles, Robert. *The Call of Service: A Witness to Idealism*. Boston: Houghton Mifflin, 1995.

Damon, William. *Greater Expectations: Overcoming the Culture of Indulgence in America's Homes and Schoools*. New York: Free Press, 1996.

Dent, Harry S. *Teaching Jack and Jill Right vs. Wrong in the Homes and Schools*. Augusta, GA: Laity Alive & Serving, Incorporated, 1996.

DeRoche, Edward F. and Mary Williams. *Educating Hearts and Minds: A comprehensive Character Education Framework*. Thousand Oaks, CA: Corwin Press, Inc., 1998.

Devine, Tony, Ho Joon Seuk, and Andrew Wilson, eds., *Cultivating Heart and Character: Educating for Life's Most Essential Goals*. Chapel Hill, NC: Character Development Publishing, 2001.

Eberly, Don. *The Content of America's Character: Recovering Civic Virtue*. Lanham, MD: Madison Books, 1996.

Etzioni, Amitai. *Character Building for a Democratic, Civil Society*. Washington, DC: The Communitarian Network, 1994.

Fine, Melinda. *Habits of Mind: Struggling Over Values in America's Classrooms*. San Francisco: Jossey Bass, 1995.

Frymier, Jak. *Values on Which We Agree*. Bloomington, IN: Phi Delta Kappa, 1995.

Gibbs, John C.., Karen S. Basinger, and Dick Fuller. *Moral Maturity: Measuring the Development of Sociomoral Reflections*. Hillsdale, NJ: Lawrence Erlbaum Associates, 1992.

Glendon, Mary Ann. *Seedbeds of Virtue: sources of Competence, Character and Citizenship in American Society*. Lanham, MD: Madison Books, 1995.

Greer, Colin and Herbert Kohl. *A Call to Character: A Family Treasury of Stories, Poems, Plays, Proverbs, and Fables to Guide the Development of Values for You and Your Children*. New York: Harper Collins, 1995.

Huffman, Henry A. *Developing a Character Education Program: One School District's Experience.* Arlington, VA: ASCD and CEP, 1994.

Hunter, James Davidson. *The Death of Character: Moral Education in an Age Without Good and Evil.* New York: Basic Books, 2000.

Kidder, Rushworth M. *How Good People Make Tough Choices: Resolving the Dilemmas of Ethical Living.* New York: Simon and Schuster, 1996.

Kurtines, William and Jacob L. Gewirtz. *Handbood of Moral Behavior and Development.* Hillsdale, NJ: Lawrence Erlbaum Associates, 1991.

Leming, James S. *Character Education: Lessons from the Past, Models for the Future.* Camden, ME: The Institute for Global Ethics, 1993.

Likona, Thomas. *Educating for Character: How Our Schools Can Teach Respect and Responsibility.* New York: Bantam Books, 1991.

Murphy, Madonna M. *Character Education in America's Blue Ribbon Schools: Best Practices for Meeting the Challenge.* Lancaster, PA: Technomic Publishing Co., 1998.

Ryan, Kevin A. and Karen E. Bohlin. *Building Character in Schools: Practical Ways to Bring Moral Instruction to Life.* San Francisco: Jossey Bass, 1998.

Stirling, Diane, et. al. *Character Education Connections for School and Community.* Port Chester, NY: National Professional Resources, 2000.

Unell, Barbara C. *20 Teachable Virtues: Practical Ways to Pass on Lessons of Virtue and Character to Your Children.* New York: Prigee Books, 1995.

Urban, Hal. *Twenty Things I Want My Kids to Know.* Nashville, TN: Thomas Nelson Publishers, 1992.

Vincent, Phillip. *Promising Practices in Character Education: Nine Success Stories from Around the Country.* Chapel Hill, NC: Character Development Group, 1996.

Wynne, E. A. and Kevin Ryan. *Reclaiming Our Schools: A Handbook on Teaching Character, Academics, and Discipline.* New York: Merril, 1997.

Sample Timeline, Goals, and Budget

The following table was developed by Grand Forks Central High School in Grand Forks, North Dakota. In it, the goals, activities, and anticipated results of the school's character education initiative are linked to a schedule and budget.

Goal	Activities/Task	Results	Completion Date	Budget
Goal 1: Character education at GFC will include an intentional, proactive, and comprehensive approach that will promote "universal virtues" in all phases of school life.	A school profile and character information pamphlet will be developed and used for public information purposes with parents and community members.	Inform parents and community.	August 2001	$250.00
Goal 1: Character education at GFC will include an intentional, proactive, and comprehensive approach that will promote "universal virtues" in all phases of school life.	Posters will be developed to promote the six universal character virtues. Posters will be distributed throughout the building in classrooms, meeting areas, and offices.	Promote the six universal virtues throughout the school.	August 2001	$1,000.00
Goal 1: Character education at GFC will include an intentional, proactive, and comprehensive approach that will promote "universal virtues" in all phases of school life.	The walls of the main first-floor hallway will be painted using the six existing pillars to promote the universal virtues. A virtue will be painted on each pillar.	Promote the six universal virtues throughout the school.	August 2001	$200.00
Goal 1: Character education at GFC will include an intentional, proactive, and comprehensive approach that will promote "universal virtues" in all phases of school life.	Book covers will be printed and distributed to all students in English, math, and science classes.	Book covers will be used to promote the six universal virtues of character while at the same time to protect new books in these academic areas.	August 2001	$550.00
Goal 1: Character education at GFC will include an intentional, proactive, and comprehensive approach that will promote "universal virtues" in all phases of school life.	A podium banner will be designed and purchased incorporating the themes of character and excellence at Central High School.	It will be used at all formal events.	January 2002	$250.00
Goal 1: Character education at GFC will include an intentional, proactive, and comprehensive approach that will promote "universal virtues" in all phases of school life.	A banner will be designed for the commons area, promoting the six universal character virtues.	Promote the six universal virtues throughout the school.	January 2002	$200.00

Goal	Activities/Task	Results	Completion Date	Budget
Goal 1: Character education at GFC will include an intentional, proactive, and comprehensive approach that will promote "universal virtues" in all phases of school life.	Screen saver software, promoting the six character virtues, will be developed during the school year to be installed on all computers in the building.	Promote the six universal virtues throughout the school	May 2002	$500.00 for copyright and software development
Goal 1: Character education at GFC will include an intentional, proactive, and comprehensive approach that will promote "universal virtues" in all phases of school life.	Student and staff handbooks will be redesigned to incorporate the six universal character virtues.	Promote the six universal virtues throughout the school.	Staff Cover August 2001 Student Handbook August 2002	$250.00
Goal 1: Character education at GFC will include an intentional, proactive, and comprehensive approach that will promote "universal virtues" in all phases of school life.	The *Centralian* newspaper will incorporate a section in each issue on character education.	Mrs. Devine's journalism class will report on character education "happenings" in the school.	May 2002	$0.00
Goal 1: Character education at GFC will include an intentional, proactive, and comprehensive approach that will promote "universal virtues" in all phases of school life.	Each week, a character education statement will be read on the announcements.	Promote the six universal virtues throughout the school.	May 2002	$0.00
Goal 1: Character education at GFC will include an intentional, proactive, and comprehensive approach that will promote "universal virtues" in all phases of school life.	A statement about character will be developed and read prior to the beginning of all sporting events at Central High School.	"Central High School promotes six universal virtues of character that include respect, responsibility, trustworthiness, caring, fairness, and citizenship. We ask that as we enjoy the athletic ability demonstrated by these athletes tonight (today) that you demonstrate good character as you cheer your team on to victory."	Year long	$0.00
Goal 2: To develop character, GFC will provide students the opportunity to practice good character.	Students will be in-serviced in August about the six universal virtues of character and expectations for good character.	Students will demonstrate appropriate behavior at athletic contests, school pep rallies, and other school events.	August 2001	$0.00

Goal	Activities/Task	Results	Completion Date	Budget
Goal 2: To develop character, GFC will provide students the opportunity to practice good character.	Teachers will provide classroom rules and expectations that incorporate the six character virtues.	Students will practice and display good character in classes.	August 2001	$0.00
Goal 2: To develop character, GFC will provide students the opportunity to practice good character.	Students will practice good character in the hallways, commons, and other gathering places in the building.	Staff members will monitor and acknowledge good character and identify and correct poor character.	Year long	$0.00
Goal 3: Character education at GFC will strive to promote intrinsic motivation to develop good character.	Students will receive information about the six universal virtues of character at orientation and small class meetings at the beginning of the school year.	Students will be encouraged to practice good character habits.	Year long	$0.00
Goal 3: Character education at GFC will strive to promote intrinsic motivation to develop good character.	The student council will be in-serviced at their first meeting about the character initiative at Central.	Leaders of student council will become the mentors of good character for other students.	Year long	$0.00
Goal 3: Character education at GFC will strive to promote intrinsic motivation to develop good character.	A speaker will meet with the student body on October 24, 2001, to talk about good character. Scott Greenberg, a national youth speaker, will be at Central on this day. He will be incorporating the six universal virtues of character into his presentation.	Promote the six universal virtues throughout the school.	October 2001	$500.00 Renaissance and student council funds will cover additional costs.
Goal 4: The staff and parents at GFC will share the responsibility for character education and attempt to adhere to the same core virtues that guide the education of students. Staff and students will share the responsibility to demonstrate character leadership during the school day.	Teacher workshop on August 24, 2001—teachers will be presented with information about character education and the promotion of the six universal virtues in their classes.	This will be an introduction to the character education initiative at Central.	August 2001	$0.00
Goal 4: The staff and parents at GFC will share the responsibility for character education and attempt to adhere to the same core virtues that guide the	Coaches and advisors will be in-serviced at the pre-school year meeting at Central.	Promote the six universal virtues throughout the school.	August 2001	$0.00

Goal	Activities/Task	Results	Completion Date	Budget
education of students. Staff and students will share the responsibility to demonstrate character leadership during the school day.				
Goal 4: The staff and parents at GFC will share the responsibility for character education and attempt to adhere to the same core virtues that guide the education of students. Staff and students will share the responsibility to demonstrate character leadership during the school day.	A presentation will be made to the Central Booster Club at the September meeting.	Promote the six universal virtues throughout the school.	August 2001	$0.00
Goal 4: The staff and parents at GFC will share the responsibility for character education and attempt to adhere to the same core virtues that guide the education of students. Staff and students will share the responsibility to demonstrate character leadership during the school day.	Teachers will be participating in in-service activities with district character education consultant B. David Brooks in September.	Promote the six universal virtues throughout the school and to answer questions teachers might have about character education.	September 2001	District Level
Goal 4: The staff and parents at GFC will share the responsibility for character education and attempt to adhere to the same core virtues that guide the education of students. Staff and students will share the responsibility to demonstrate character leadership during the school day.	A parent meeting will be held in September in the school auditorium with B. David Brooks.	Inform parents and community.	September 2001	District Level
Goal 5: Evaluation of character education at GFC will assess the school climate to the extent in which students manifest good character and the staff and parents function as character education mentors.	The character education committee will be developing an assessment tool during the 2001-2002 school year.	Baseline data is developed to provide assessment of overall impact of the character education initiative at Central.	Survey developed by March 2002. Survey is given in April 2002; Results by June 2002.	$300.00 for UND Bureau of Statistics services.

TOTAL BUDGET COSTS   **$4,000.00**

Reprinted with permission by Grand Forks Central High School, Grand Forks, ND.

A

"ABC" questions 86–89
ACT 89–93
Adams, Samuel 155
adult modeling/behavior 30–31, 54–55, 57, 80, 118–119, 127, 148, 160
advertising 71–73, 106–107, 108, 109, 113, 114, 157
Advocate, The 118–119
Aesop 137
alcohol use/abuse 4, 19, 25
Allen, Dick 133
alternatives 86–89
anecdotal reports 138, 139–141, 152
announcements 117–118, 158, 166
Annual Stakeholder Satisfaction Survey 141–142
assessment 56–64, 125–141
Association of Supervision and Curriculum Development (ASCD) 9
Atascocita Middle School (TX) 96, 117
Atlantis Elementary School (FL) 108
attitudes/perceptions 29–30, 31, 32–34, 56–57, 62, 63–64, 71, 118
Auburn University 73

B

Baraquio, Angela Perez 14
basic principles (*see* core values)
Baumeister, Roy 22
Beck, Mike 94
belief statement 39, 49, 50
Bellah, Robert 22
Bennett, William 20, 118–119
Blume, Cathy 149
board of education 13, 17, 35, 38, 47, 122, 129
Booz, David 79, 80
Bronowski, Jacob 99
budget 41, 45, 46, 180–183
bullying 20, 24
Bush, George W. 14, 74

C

California Partnership in Character Education 74
Case for Character Education, The 7
case study 15–17, 33–34, 49–51, 63–64, 79–81, 97, 120–122, 133–135, 152–153, 165–166
Castle, Annie 97

Centennial Intermediate School (CA) 77
Center for Child and Family Studies (University of South Carolina) 137
Character Counts! Coalition 9
Character Counts! Midshore 133–135
character education organizations 8–9, 174–175
Character Education Partnership (CEP) 8–9, 14, 75, 142–143
Character Education Network of the ASCD 9
Character Education Survey 57, 62, 170–171
character moment 116–117, 157
Character Education Quality Standards 142–144
cheating 24–25, 58
church (*see* religion)
Cianfrani, Donna 68
classroom strategies 148–150
climate 53–64, 65, 75, 76, 100–103, 115, 120
clubs 163
College of Social Work (University of South Carolina) 149
communication 47–49, 100, 123–135
community involvement 128–135, 162–164
conflict resolution 11, 12, 16, 59, 71, 79, 84, 85, 88–89
consequences 86–89, 96, 101
Content of America's Character, The 9
core values/core consensus values 7, 10, 11, 17, 22, 51, 53, 73, 75, 129, 143
Cotswold Elementary School (NC) 68
critics 8, 49, 124–125
Crosby Independent School District (TX) 97
Cultivating Heart and Character 22
culture 13, 14, 53, 71, 75, 100, 101, 103, 107, 108, 113, 115, 117, 118, 120
curriculum infusion/integration 13, 40, 60, 96, 144

D

decision-making 83–97
Dent, Harry S. 19
Delattre, Edwin J. 118–119
DeRoche, Edward F. 35, 48
DeVargas, Robert C. 148, 149
DeVargas Study 148, 149
directive moral education 5
District of Columbia 14
dropouts 4, 8
drug use/abuse 4, 8, 19

E

Easton, MD 134
Eberly, D.E. 9
Educating for Character 8, 9
Educating Hearts and Minds 48–49
Education Commission of the States 14
Eleven Principles of Effective Character Education 9–10, 143
Emperor Elementary School (CA) 60
environment 99, 100–106
Ethical Relativism: Teaching the Virtues 4
evaluation 10, 11, 46, 137–153
Excelsior High School (CA) 140–141
expectations 71, 101, 112–114, 118
extracurricular activities 152–154

F

fair play (*see* sportsmanship)
family (*see* parent)
funding 46, 176–177

G

gangs 4, 8, 19, 34
goals/goal setting 39, 41, 42–46, 49, 50–51
Grand Forks Public Schools (ND) 146
guidance 152–154
Gulf Middle School (FL) 108

H

Hackley, Lloyd V. 22
Hedgepeth, Vicki 75
Humble Character Development Program 15, 17, 51
Humble ISD (TX) 15, 49–51, 97, 120–122
Humble Ninth Grade School (TX) 92
Hurley, Michael 53

I

I-ACT 92–93
in-service training 64, 100, 121, 122
intervention/intervention programs 6
invisible curriculum 8, 100

J

Jordan-Hare Stadium 73

K

Kingwood Middle School (TX) 61, 145

L

language 65–71, 75, 81, 106–108, 115, 117, 118, 119, 156–157, 164
languaging 65, 67, 71, 73, 90
Lasch, Christopher 22
Leesville Middle School (NC) 75
legislation 74
Lein, Mary 146
Lein Study 146, 149
Lessons in Character 59, 145, 146, 148
Lickert Scale 29
Lickona, Thomas 9, 74, 77
literal thinkers/thinking 67–69
Little Engine That Could, The 5
Los Angeles County 32
Los Angeles County Office of Education 5
Los Angeles Unified School District 70, 141, 146, 147
lying 25

M

measurement (*see* evaluation)
media/mass media 129, 131
metacognition 95
mission statement/vision statement 45, 50
modeling (*see* adult modeling/behavior)
Monk, Doug 61, 62, 145, 149
Monk Study 145, 149
moral relativism 4

N

Nairn, Camille S. 149
"Nine Essential Elements for Success" 39–40
New Orleans Parish Schools 84

P

Paget, Kathy 149
parent
    involvement 118, 123–129, 162–163
    communication with 118–120, 162–163, 167–168
perceptions (*see* attitudes and perceptions)
Perini, Kathy 61
planning 35–51
Positive Model for Change (PMFC) 27–29
posters 158, 161
practice(s) 11, 12, 16, 71, 77–78, 83
prevention 6

principle(s) 11, 16–17, 71, 73–76, 83, 84
process 12–13, 16, 71, 78–79, 83–97
Puerto Rico 14

Q

quasi-scientific studies 138, 139, 141–142, 145–149, 152–153

R

recognition 115, 163, 164, 165–166,
religion/religious beliefs 3, 7, 37, 124, 128, 132
Report Card on the Ethics of American Youth, The 24
resistance 36, 109, 124–125
resolving conflicts (*see* conflict resolution)
REVIEW 93–96, 97, 126
Roosevelt, Franklin Delano 82
runaways 4
Ryan, Kevin 77

S

San Gabriel, CA 60
San Marcos Midddle School (CA) 85
Santa Barbara High School (CA) 76
schedule (*see* timeline)
school as island 75, 107–108, 118
school board (*see* board of education)
school culture (*see* culture)
school-to-work 13
school-wide strategies 144-147
scientific studies 138, 142–143, 152
Scottsdale, AZ 36
Senate Bill 311 74
Seuk, Ho Joon 22
signage 108–112, 127, 128, 158, 159, 160, 161
"Six-Pillars of Character" 16, 17, 51, 74
Sociomoral Reflective Measure–Short Form 148
Sommers, Christina 4–5
South Carolina Partnership in Character Education 150–152
South Carolina State Department of Education 149
South Carroll High School (MD) 79–81
sportsmanship 74, 129, 134, 161
stakeholder(s) 31, 32, 35, 36, 37, 41, 47, 49, 54–56
S.T.A.R. 16, 17, 79, 81–97, 126
steering committee 15, 35–51, 56, 58, 61, 79, 81–97, 99, 120, 155
STOP 84–86
strategic plan 42, 45, 96, 99

stealing 25
student planners/agendas 147, 159
Styles, David 134
systematic character education 7–8, 9, 14, 38, 39, 45, 47, 54, 56, 57, 58, 59, 103, 104, 107, 124

T

"Take 5 for Character" 134
teen pregnancy 4, 8
THINK 86–89
Thompson, Mona 96
Thorfinnson Study 145
Thorfinnson, Tana R. 145
Three P's 11, 53, 57, 71–73, 83
timeline 121–122, 180–184
Tucson, AZ 37

U

United States Department of Education 4
University of South Carolina 149
Urban, Hal 65

V

values clarification 4–6, 8
values education 7
victim thinking 89–93
Vincent, Phil 77
violence 19, 20, 25
vision statement (*see* mission statement)

W

Westerfeld, Ron 117
Whitworth, Rosemarie 85–86
Williams, Mary M. 35, 48, 77
Wilson, Andrew 22
Word of the Week program 145
workplace skills 130, 132, 135
Wulf, Kathleen M. 146
Wulf Study 146–148, 149